WAGE BEHAVIOR
IN THE POSTWAR PERIOD

An Empirical Analysis

Wage Behavior in the Postwar Period

An Empirical Analysis S

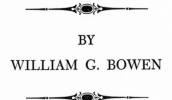

BY

WILLIAM G. BOWEN

1960

INDUSTRIAL RELATIONS SECTION

Department of Economics

PRINCETON UNIVERSITY

Princeton, New Jersey, U.S.A.

INDUSTRIAL RELATIONS SECTION
Department of Economics
PRINCETON UNIVERSITY
Established 1922

FREDERICK HARBISON, *Director*
HAZEL C. BENJAMIN, *Librarian*
NELLIE OFFUTT, *Administrative Assistant*
DORIS MCBRIDE, *Secretary*

———————

J. DOUGLAS BROWN, *Faculty Associate*
RICHARD A. LESTER, *Faculty Associate*
WILBERT E. MOORE, *Faculty Associate*

The reports of the Industrial Relations Section are the joint product of the Section's staff under the supervision of the Director. In the case of each report, the research and preparation of manuscript is done by the staff member whose name appears on the title page.

Research Report Series No. 100

FOREWORD

THE analysis of wage behavior and its relation to prices and inflation has been a continuing interest of Professor William G. Bowen and other members of the Industrial Relations Section staff. The first study, published last year, sets forth a complete theoretical analysis of wage-price relationships in modern economic society.* In this second study, *Wage Behavior in the Postwar Period*, Professor Bowen has made a thorough examination of the actual behavior of wages in relation to the inflation problem. He presents new information on how wages have behaved since World War II, and examines rigorously the role of such factors as unemployment, escalator contracts, unionization, industrial concentration, and profits in determining wage levels.

For those who have been concerned with wage behavior in recent decades, this volume offers both surprises and confirmation of widely-held beliefs. Among the more important findings are the following: unemployment and wages are much more loosely related than has usually been assumed; small changes in the level of unemployment seem to have little effect on the pace at which wages increase; wages have gone up faster at given levels of unemployment in the postwar period than in earlier years; unions appear to have had more pronounced effects on wages in prosperous times than in recessions (the exact opposite of the commonly held view); industrial concentration appears to be a major factor holding wages up in time of recession; and the relatively rapid rate of wage increase in the 1958 recession can be attributed, at least in part, to the timing of key long-term agreements and to the fact that the brunt of the 1958 recession fell on what Bowen calls the "market-power" sector.

The findings of this study have important implications for public policy. In particular, they provide the kind of empirical

* William G. Bowen, *The Wage-Price Issue*, Princeton University Press, Princeton. 1960.

v

Foreword

evidence which is necessary to determine the probable cost, in terms of inflation, of maintaining high employment. Thus, this volume can be read with profit by all those who are concerned with public policy as related to inflation, unemployment, and wage and price relationships.

FREDERICK HARBISON
Director

Princeton, New Jersey
September 15, 1960

PREFACE

THIS is primarily an empirical study of wage behavior in the postwar period. I have had ample opportunity to comment elsewhere on the purely theoretical aspects of wage behavior and on the *a priori* relationships between wage behavior, price behavior, and the inflation problem; and a determined effort has been made to avoid repeating this earlier theoretical work here. Theoretical analysis does, however, appear in those places where *a priori* reasoning must be used to explain why certain empirical questions were asked and why certain interpretations were made.

Since the focus of this study is the role of wage behavior in the inflationary process, at various places in the text it will appear as if I am suggesting that large wage increases are "bad" and small wage increases are "good." Needless to say, utterances of this sort should not be construed as a general condemnation of high wages. In contexts other than the inflation problem, large wage increases might be regarded as highly desirable; however, this particular study abstracts altogether from questions of income distribution, economic efficiency, and equity.

The results of this empirical investigation of wage behavior are dependent on a number of important methodological decisions. While a sincere attempt has been made to prevent purely methodological discussions from obscuring the flow of the analysis, occasional references to methodology do occur in the text, and a more complete discussion of certain methodological aspects of the study appears in the Appendixes. To carry out this study it was necessary to collect data from widely varied sources and to perform a number of manipulations in order to render the data useable. Consequently, to offer the reader an opportunity to examine the empirical basis on which the conclusions of this study rest, several sets of data relating to wages,

Preface

profits, employment, unionization, and concentration are also presented in the Appendixes.

In the preparation of this study I have received financial support not only from the Industrial Relations Section of Princeton University but also from the Commission on Money and Credit and from the Ford Foundation's grant to Princeton University to support economic research. The Commission on Money and Credit deserves special mention in that it financed the writing of the first draft of this report as well as a considerable amount of the underlying research. However, the Commission should in no way be identified with any findings contained in this monograph.

A number of statistical series used in this study had to be specially constructed, and much early work of this type must be credited to the patient efforts of Mr. N. D. Brown. In the subsequent stages of the study Mr. R. A. Berry provided invaluable research assistance, and the detailed calculations on which many of the conclusions of this report are based must be attributed directly to his careful and highly competent work. Thanks are also due to Mrs. D. H. Bayley for drawing the charts and to Mrs. D. H. Lake for doing the bulk of the typing.

Finally, I am indebted to my colleagues, and particularly to S. T. Beza, L. V. Chandler, R. A. Lester, J. W. Markham, and R. E. Quandt, for numerous comments and helpful suggestions. Needless to say, none of these men can be held responsible for any errors or maljudgments that remain in the final product.

WILLIAM G. BOWEN

Princeton, New Jersey
September 15, 1960

viii

CONTENTS

Contents

Contents

LIST OF TABLES

LIST OF CHARTS

I. INTRODUCTION: THE GENERAL ROLE OF WAGE BEHAVIOR IN THE INFLATIONARY PROCESS

IN recent years, wage behavior has come to occupy a central place in discussions of the inflation problem. Today it is generally recognized that wage behavior is an important determinant of the degree of success we can expect from monetary-fiscal policies aimed at the simultaneous attainment of the twin goals of price stability and high employment.

Wages and prices are, of course, related in many diverse and complicated ways. For present purposes, it is convenient to draw a rough-and-ready distinction between what may be called the wage determination aspect of the wage-price relationship and what may be called the cost and price determination aspects. The wage determination aspect is concerned with the magnitude of wage adjustments and with the effect of such factors as unemployment, unionization, and industrial concentration on the size of wage adjustments. The cost and price determination aspects of the wage-price relationship are, on the other hand, concerned with the effects of a *given* change in money wages on labor costs and total costs as well as with the effects of costs on prices.

This monograph is concerned solely with the wage determination aspect of the relationship between wage behavior and inflation, and does not consider the consequences of given wage adjustments for costs and prices. The purposes of this monograph are to analyze in some detail the actual behavior of money wages in the United States during the postwar years and to spell out the implications of this pattern of wage behavior for monetary and fiscal policies.

However, before marshalling "the facts," it is essential to know what facts are worth collecting. The main part of this introductory chapter must, therefore, be devoted to pinpoint-

Introduction

ing the basic questions about wage behavior that the remainder of the study will endeavor to answer.[1]

"Cost Inflation" Versus "Demand Inflation" and the Unemployment-Wage Relationship

The role of wage behavior in the inflationary process has so frequently been discussed in conjunction with the popular distinction between "cost inflation" and "demand inflation" that, before going any further, it is necessary to emphasize that the usual versions of this distinction do *not* provide a fruitful basis for empirical work. In brief, the position taken in this study is that the usual distinction between prices that are pulled up from the demand side and prices that are pushed up by autonomous cost pressures is misleading and unworkable for the simple reason that there is no satisfactory way of establishing how much of any given price increase is "cost-induced" and how much is "demand-induced."[2]

With respect to wage behavior, the crucial question suggested by the "cost inflation"-"demand inflation" distinction is: How much of a given wage increase is due to the upward pull of an excess demand for labor and how much is due to the "autonomous" upward pressure of trade unions? This question is simply unanswerable. The reason is that the amount of the wage increase a union demands and succeeds in obtaining is itself a function of the employer's demand for labor, his profit position, and his ability to pass on higher wages in the form of

[1] Practical considerations—mainly the pressures of time—dictated that the scope of this study be restricted to the wage determination aspect of the wage-price problem. Ideally, it would be better to investigate wage determination in conjunction with cost and price determination so that we could take proper account of the inter-relationships between wages, costs, and prices that characterize our economy. The fact that this study does not deal with all of these inter-relationships means that the empirical results presented here are subject to corresponding limitations and must therefore be interpreted carefully.

[2] For a detailed discussion of the reasoning behind this conclusion, see my " 'Cost Inflation' Versus 'Demand Inflation': A Useful Distinction?" *Southern Economic Journal*, January 1960, pp. 199-206.

Introduction

higher prices. When the collective bargaining situation and the demand for labor are this inter-related there is simply no way of finding out how much of the final wage increase was "demand-induced" and how much was "autonomous."

Our inability to tell precisely what portion of a wage increase is due exclusively to the mechanism of collective bargaining and what portion is due exclusively to the demand for labor does not, however, mean that empirical investigations of wage behavior have nothing to contribute to the formulation of anti-inflation policies. To argue that, because the strength of demand always plays *some* role in wage-setting, demand conditions alone are worth studying, is equally as foolish as concentrating solely on the role of unions or trying to put "demand-induced" and "autonomous" wage increases into water-tight compartments.

The essential point to be kept in mind is that wage behavior invariably depends on the interaction between aggregate demand and the characteristics of the wage-setting institutions through which changes in aggregate demand are transmitted. It is true that historically more attention has been paid to changes in aggregate demand than to the characteristics of our wage- and price-setting institutions. There are perhaps two reasons why this has been the case.

First of all, big inflations inevitably involve big increases in aggregate demand. Whereas sudden and rapid increases in aggregate demand are always a possibility, our wage- and price-setting institutions change slowly and are not likely to generate a rapid inflation in the absence of strong exogenous increases in aggregate demand. Consequently, so long as we were worried about big inflations, concentration on demand conditions was in order. It is comforting to think that at least part of our comparatively recent concern with wage- and price-setting institutions as the source of "creeping inflation" is due to the absence of bigger problems. Now that we think we know how to prevent "galloping inflation," we have turned our attention to

Introduction

the problem of "creeping inflation"—and in this context the interaction between aggregate demand and the behavior of wage- and price-setting institutions becomes much more important.

The second reason for the historical emphasis on demand as the cornerstone of the inflation problem is directly relevant to the subject matter of this monograph. Historically, economists have been more inclined to assume the general existence of perfect competition than they are today, when we are constantly aware of both the existence and importance of big business and big labor. From the standpoint of the inflation question, the significance of the perfect competition assumption is that it permits us to ignore the behavior patterns of individual wage- and price-setters and to concentrate instead on the level of aggregate demand.

Under conditions of perfect competition, wages and prices are, of course, sensitive to changes in aggregate demand; furthermore, whenever there is an excess supply of anything, the price of that thing will fall. Consequently, if there were perfect competition in all markets, there would never be any need to worry about the *simultaneous* occurrence of unemployment and inflation. The existence of inflation would imply an excess of aggregate demand, and with excess demand there would not be unemployment; the existence of unemployment would imply excess supply, prices and wages would fall, and so inflation could not accompany unemployment. In a perfectly competitive world, the task of monetary-fiscal policy would thus be comparatively simple: by regulating the level of aggregate demand it would be possible to pursue the goals of price stability and full employment without fear that the achievement of one goal would necessitate the sacrifice of the other.

We do not, of course, live in a perfectly competitive world. Nonetheless, the nature of wage behavior in a perfectly competitive world does provide valuable insights into both the

Introduction

conditions that are necessary for wage behavior to play an important role in the inflationary process and the empirical questions about wage behavior that are worth asking. In terms of structure, we know that atomistic wage-setting should not cause inflation problems (although it may cause other kinds of problems) and that it takes the existence of market power in the labor market to make wage behavior of interest to the student of inflation.

In terms of performance, the perfectly competitive world provides an even more significant guide-line: Wage behavior deserves to occupy an important role in the analysis of the inflationary process only to the extent that wages are not sensitive to demand and supply conditions in the labor market (approximated by the unemployment percentage) and do not stop rising when there is unemployment.

The important point is that the contribution of wage behavior to the policy dilemma facing monetary-fiscal policy (namely, that the goals of price stability and full employment are incompatible and that we must decide how intensely to pursue each goal) depends directly on the flexibility of wages with respect to the level of unemployment. Consequently, to study the role of wage behavior in the inflationary process, one must study the behavior of wages in close conjunction with the behavior of unemployment. *The relationship between unemployment and the rate at which money wages rise is the key empirical relationship.*[1]

[1] When it is necessary to specify the direction of causation implied in the relationship between money wages and unemployment, we shall follow the usual practice of treating unemployment as a determinant of wage behavior and assuming that money wage behavior does not react back on the level of unemployment. As long as changes in the price level do not exert a significant effect on spending plans by altering the real value of people's wealth, and as long as monetary-fiscal policies are not themselves determined to a significant extent by the inflation-unemployment milieu, this treatment seems reasonable. Except in special cases, a (small) change in the level of money wages should not be expected to have a marked effect on the level of employment.

Introduction

*The Basic Questions To Be Answered
and Their Significance*

The basic empirical questions that grow out of this key relationship between unemployment and money wage adjustments, and the significance of these questions, can be summarized as follows:

1. Does the rate at which wages increase seem to depend on the level of unemployment, and if so, how fast do wages rise at various levels of unemployment?

> *Significance.*—Will provide at least a rough idea of the "terms-of-trade" between unemployment and wage increases, and will help us determine how much unemployment is necessary to prevent wages from rising faster than productivity, and to what extent high employment policies are likely to accentuate the rate at which money wages rise.

2. How "loose" is the relationship between unemployment and the rate of wage increase? How large is the range of wage adjustments associated with a given amount of unemployment?

> *Significance.*—Tells us how confident we can be that the "normal" wage increase will be associated with a given amount of unemployment; also provides information as to the overall importance of factors *other than unemployment* in determining wages and thus gives us some idea of the extent to which it is possible to influence wages without altering the level of unemployment.

3. Has there been any trend in the relationship between the level of unemployment and the rate of wage increase over time? Is the same amount of unemployment associated with larger wage increases at the present than in the past?

Introduction

Significance.—Will help determine if our wage-setting institutions seem to be changing so as to make the dilemma between price stability and high employment more acute.

4. When the level of unemployment is held constant, what are the effects on wages of various other factors, and do these effects depend on the level at which unemployment is held constant? Specifically, how is the rate of wage increase affected by:

a) The direction in which unemployment is changing—that is, do wages go up faster when unemployment is decreasing than when unemployment is increasing?

b) Changes in production worker employment and the distribution of these changes among various kinds of industries?

c) Changes in the general level of profits and the distribution of profits among various kinds of industries?

d) Changes in the general price level itself?

e) The pattern of unionization among industries?

f) The pattern of industrial concentration among industries?

g) The length of collective bargaining agreements?

Significance.—Will improve our ability to predict the relationship between unemployment and wages under differing conditions; will also tell us what effects policies aimed at wage-determining factors other than the level of unemployment are likely to have on the pace of wage increases.

These, then, are the questions that this study will endeavor to answer. The organization of the succeeding chapters parallels the above list of questions, except that the detailed analysis of wage behavior in the 1947-59 period is preceded by a brief

Introduction

examination of the unemployment-wage relationship over the entire period from 1900 to 1957.

Before plunging into the main body of the analysis, it is, however, necessary to pause briefly and consider the problem of occupational differences in wage behavior.

Occupational Differences in Wage Behavior

Thus far wage behavior has been discussed as if there were a single wage statistic representative of wages paid to workers in all occupations, industries, and geographical locations. Unfortunately, there is no such ideal wage statistic. While it is possible to construct an aggregate wage index that is useful in some connections, most of the empirical results of this study will be based on average hourly earnings paid production workers in manufacturing industries. It must be emphasized that the selection of average hourly earnings paid production workers as the main wage variable is dictated largely by practical considerations and is not meant to imply that all other wages and salaries are of no consequence for the inflation problem.

In order to provide perspective on the production worker wage data that will be used so extensively, it may be helpful at this juncture to look briefly at the differences in wage and employment behavior between production workers and other broad occupational categories over the 1950-58 period.

The Bureau of the Census data on median annual wage or salary incomes presented in Table 1 indicate the diversity in income and employment trends among the various occupational groups. One noteworthy fact is that the two occupational groups that experienced the most rapid increases in income between 1950 and 1958 (professional-technical workers and clerical workers) are salaried employees and are *not* in the production worker categories.[1] A third salaried group (managers

[1] The three occupational groups that can be considered production workers are labelled (P) in the left margin of Table 1.

Introduction

and officials) experienced a more rapid increase in incomes than did the semi-skilled and unskilled production workers.

The implication of these occupational income data is that the earnings gains of production workers did not exceed the earnings gains of salaried workers as a group; in fact, if any positive conclusion suggests itself, it is that the earnings of salaried workers went up faster than the earnings of production workers.[1] Other studies, confined to manufacturing, support this general conclusion. Conrad, for example, found that the average annual earnings of nonproduction workers rose about 5 percent more rapidly over the decade 1947-56 than did the average annual earnings of production workers, and that the relatively faster increase in salaries has been particularly pronounced in the years since 1953.[2] These figures suggest that the rates of increase in average hourly earnings that will be cited throughout this study are more likely to understate than to exaggerate the rates at which wages and salaries in toto have increased.

The occupational employment data contained in Table 1 are as significant as the income figures. Apart from the phenomenal 49.9% increase in professional-technical workers, the most striking aspect of the inter-occupational employment data is the decline in the employment of production workers that occurred alongside the expansion in the employment of white-collar personnel. This is simply evidence of the marked increase in the proportion of white-collar workers in the labor force that

[1] The use of 1950 as the base date and 1958 as the terminal date for these comparisons requires that care be exercised in interpreting the precise inter-occupational differences in the speed with which earnings in different occupations rose. However, the substitution of 1956 for the recession year of 1958 as the terminal date for the comparisons does not alter the ranking of the occupations with respect to changes in income in any significant way.

[2] Alfred H. Conrad, "The Share of Wages and Salaries in Manufacturing Incomes, 1947-56," Study Paper No. 9, Joint Economic Committee, 86th Cong., 1st Sess., 1959, p. 142. For similar findings, see: Charles L. Schultze, "Recent Inflation in the United States," Study Paper No. 1, Joint Economic Committee, 86th Cong., 1st Sess., 1959, pp. 2, 10ff.

TABLE 1
INCOME AND EMPLOYMENT DATA, BY OCCUPATIONAL GROUP*
1950-58

Occupational Group	Percentage Increase In Median Wage or Salary Income 1950-58	Percentage Increase In Total Employment 1950-58	Total Number of Persons Earning Income in 1958 (in thousands)
Professional, technical, and kindred workers	53.7	49.9	4,411
Clerical and kindred workers	46.5	11.3	2,902
(P) Craftsmen, foremen, and kindred workers	46.0	−1.3	8,152
Managers, officials, and propr's, except farm	44.7	11.0	5,665
(P) Operatives and kindred workers	42.9	−4.7	8,270
Sales workers	36.3	11.9	2,663
Service workers, except private household	34.4	11.6	2,682
(P) Laborers, except farm and mine	34.4	−9.6	3,322
Farm laborers and foremen	−23.9	−10.2	1,175

* Income and employment data cover only male members of the experienced civilian labor force.
Source: Compiled from U.S. Department of Commerce, Bureau of the Census, *Current Population Reports*, Series P-60, no. 33, pp. 6, 40; no. 9, p. 36.

Introduction

has been so widely recognized and discussed. While workers in the production worker categories still comprise nearly half of total male employment (see the third column of Table 1), it is important to remember that the production worker wage data presented on subsequent pages of this monograph represent a segment of the labor force that is declining in relative importance. Unfortunately, the dearth of useable salary data makes it extremely difficult to give salaried employees proper attention in studies of wage behavior.

Finally, looking at the income and employment changes in conjunction with one another, it is worth noting that the relatively faster increase in the money incomes of salaried employees can quite plausibly be explained in terms of the relatively faster increase in the employment of salaried workers compared to production workers. In fact, in light of the marked disparity between employment trends in these two broad areas of the labor force, it is surprising that the relative increase in the incomes of salaried workers has not been even greater.

II. SOME HISTORICAL PERSPECTIVE: UNEMPLOYMENT AND WAGES 1900-1958

HAVE wages in the postwar years behaved in a markedly different fashion from wages in earlier periods of our history? Does the postwar tendency of wages to rise faster than output per man-hour signal some new development in our economy? To answer these familiar questions concerning the alleged novelty of the wage determination aspects of our postwar inflation problem, it is necessary to look briefly at the historical behavior of money wages in the United States. An examination of wage behavior alone, however, will not tell us very much, since a more rapid rate of wage increase in recent years might be due entirely to the fact that the average level of unemployment has been lower in the postwar period than in prewar years. As was emphasized in Chapter I, the contribution of wage behavior to the inflation problem can be ascertained only by examining wage behavior in conjunction with unemployment conditions, and therefore it is the historical relationship between unemployment conditions and the rate of change of money wages that constitutes the subject-matter of this chapter.

Unfortunately, our ability to conduct this type of historical inquiry is seriously limited by shortages of data, methodological problems, and the lack of truly comparable periods. Useful monthly data do not antedate the postwar period, and annual unemployment data are available only from 1900 to the present. The fact that we are forced to use annual data raises a troublesome methodological problem concerning the way we gear together unemployment data for a given year with wage data that measure the rate of change of money wages *between* two years. And, the niggardliness of nature in supplying us with comparable time periods is the most serious problem of all. When one subtracts from the twentieth century the years

Unemployment and Wages: 1900-1958

marked by two world wars and the most severe depression in our history, there are not many "normal" periods left. Furthermore, the comparability of these "normal" years is marred by such far-reaching economic factors as the reduction in immigration and the rapid trend from farm to factory.

While these limitations make the projection of detailed historical data exceedingly hazardous, it is still possible to reach general conclusions concerning both the historical relationship between unemployment and money wage increases and the question of whether or not this long-term relationship has shifted significantly in recent years.[1]

The Long-Term Relationship
Between Unemployment and Wages

The relationship between unemployment as a percentage of the nonfarm work-force and the annual percentage increase in the average hourly earnings of manufacturing production workers is depicted in Chart 1. (The years from 1947 through 1958 have been circled for later reference.)[2] A person taking a quick

[1] Since the primary focus of this study is on the postwar period, only the main substantive conclusions stemming from an analysis of the historical relationship between money wages and unemployment are presented in this chapter. The author plans to prepare a separate paper containing a much more detailed discussion of the results of this historical analysis. A number of detailed studies of the historical unemployment-wage relationship in the United Kingdom are already available, and one of the reasons for preparing a separate paper on this topic is so that experience in the U.S. can be compared with experience in the U.K. In the interests of conciseness, no references to the British studies are included in this monograph.

[2] Appendix A contains the data plotted on this chart as well as an explanation of the sources of the data. One important point to note about this scattergram is that the percentage wage change indicated for a given year (t) is defined as $\dfrac{W_{t+1} - W_t}{W_t}$. Since the wage figure for a given year must be taken to represent the wage at the mid-point of that year, this convention means that the wage change indicated for 1916, for example, really represents the wage change that occurred between mid-1916 and mid-1917. This amounts to introducing a six-month lag into the relationship between unemployment and wage changes. While this treatment is not free from conceptual disadvantages it does seem

Unemployment and Wages: 1900-1958

CHART 1
RELATIONSHIP BETWEEN NONFARM UNEMPLOYMENT AND ANNUAL CHANGES IN MONEY WAGES
1900-1958

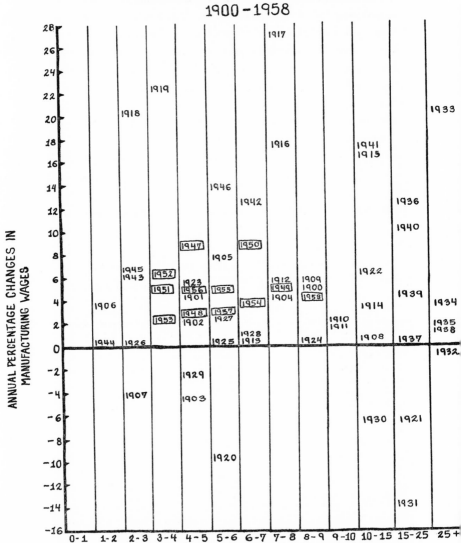

Unemployment and Wages: 1900-1958

glance at this scattergram could certainly be excused for failing to note *any* relationship between annual unemployment and annual changes in money wages. Closer scrutiny indicates, however, that there is at least a weak relationship and that it is in the expected direction: Wages have gone up faster when unemployment is relatively low than when unemployment is relatively high. The correlation between unemployment and wage changes is negative, indicating the expected inverse relationship.

The negative relationship between wage changes and degree of unemployment is certainly not very strong, however. The "average" change in money wages associated with different levels of unemployment can perhaps be seen more clearly in Table 2 than in the scattergram. The tendency of wages to go up faster when unemployment is relatively low than when un-

TABLE 2

MEDIAN PERCENTAGE WAGE CHANGES AND THE RATE OF
UNEMPLOYMENT OF NONFARM EMPLOYEES, 1900-1958

Percent Unemployed	Median Percentage Wage Change	Number of Observations
0-1	—	0
1-2	2.0	2
2-3	6.0	5
3-4	5.5	4
4-5	4.0	8
5-6	2.9	7
6-7	3.9	5
7-8	5.7	5
8-9	4.3	4
9-10	1.7	2
10-15	4.7	6
15-25	2.5	6
25+	1.1	5

Source: Appendix A.

superior to either of the other two main alternatives: introducing a six-month *lead* into the unemployment-wage relationship (so that the wage change between mid-1916 and mid-1917 is correlated with unemployment in 1917) or averaging the wage or unemployment data.

15

Unemployment and Wages: 1900-1958

employment is relatively high is most noticeable in the 2-6% range of unemployment. As the level of unemployment goes up from 2-3% to 5-6%, the median rate of wage increase declines steadily from 6.0% to 5.5% to 4.0% to 2.9%. However, once we leave the 2-6% range of unemployment, the median wage changes jump around considerably more; there is certainly no steady decline in the rate of wage increase as the level of unemployment rises. In fact, the median wage increase was larger when unemployment was between 6-7%, 7-8%, and 8-9% than when unemployment was between 4-5% and 5-6%.

Much more noticeable than the slight negative correlation between wage changes and unemployment is the extreme looseness of the entire relationship. A part of the looseness that is so apparent in the scattergram is no doubt due to the extremely large wage increases associated with the first world war and to the abnormally large wage increases that occurred in some depression years as a consequence of the N.I.R.A. and related recovery efforts. However, even after the extremely large wage increases are removed from the data, the correlation is still very low.[1] Another indication of the looseness of the relationship is the tremendous range of the wage increases associated with a given level of nonfarm unemployment. For example, when nonfarm unemployment was 4-5%, we had wage increases ranging from 9.1% in 1947 to −4.5% in 1903; when nonfarm unemployment was 8-9%, wage increases ranged from 5.7% in 1909 to 0.0% in 1924.

In light of the extreme looseness of this historical relationship (coupled with the data, methodology, and comparability problems noted earlier), any precise, mechanistic projection of these historical data would be very risky indeed. Nonethe-

[1] If we exclude all wage increases larger than 10%/annum, $r = -.18$ and the 95% confidence interval is $-.43 \leq r \leq .07$. At the 5% level of significance, r would have to equal at least $\pm .29$ to allow us to reject the null hypothesis that $r = 0$. If no wage data are excluded, $r = -.04$ and the 95% confidence interval is $-.30 \leq r \leq .22$.

Unemployment and Wages: 1900-1958

level of unemployment prevailed. In the 4-5% unemployment interval, the median wage increase that occurred in the three recent years represented in this interval is clearly higher than the median wage increase that occurred in the five earlier years. When unemployment was between 5% and 6%, the wage increases in the two recent years were larger than the wage increases in three of the four prewar years. In the 6-7% unemployment interval, both postwar years witnessed larger wage increases than the two prewar years. And, in both the 7-8% and 8-9% unemployment intervals, the same pattern repeats itself: the median wage increase in the recent period is above the median wage increase in the earlier part of the century.[1]

We must be very careful not to misinterpret the results of this comparison. While it is clear that there has been *some* upward shift in the unemployment-wage relationship over time, the magnitude of this shift must not be exaggerated. In particular, it must be recognized that the long-term tendency for wages to rise regardless of the amount of unemployment is *not* attributable solely to recent wage behavior. A recomputation of Table 2 (comparing the median wage increase to the level of nonfarm unemployment) based solely on experience prior to the end of World War II shows that the median rate of wage

[1] Again, it may be noted that these results are not altered significantly if the more familiar total civilian labor force unemployment series is substituted for the nonfarm unemployment series—the main difference is simply that all the wage adjustments would be associated with lower levels of unemployment, since the percentage of the civilian labor force unemployed is always smaller than the percentage of nonfarm employees unemployed. The nonfarm series has an important advantage in drawing historical comparisons, since it tends to allow for the very sizeable shift from farm to nonfarm employment that has occurred in this century. The upward shift in the unemployment-wage relationship can also be seen by comparing regression lines fitted to the recent period and to the period 1900-1958. The regression line representing wage behavior in the recent period is everywhere above the regression line for the entire 1900-1958 period. Finally, it is worth noting that the wage data used here do not include "fringe benefits," and thus understate the true upward shift in the unemployment-wage relationship since wages plus fringe benefits have increased more rapidly over time than wages alone.

Unemployment and Wages: 1900-1958

increase is still positive regardless of the level of unemployment. It is true, however, that the tendency of money wages to rise faster than 2.5%/annum, regardless of the level of unemployment, has been more pronounced in the recent period.

Finally, it is worth re-emphasizing that all of the above historical comparisons are, of necessity, based on annual data. Consequently, it has not been possible to take into account the possibility of short time lags or to compare wage behavior over various phases of the business cycle. To remedy these difficulties—as well as to permit examination of the impact of factors other than the level of unemployment on wage behavior—the detailed analysis of the 1947-59 period contained in the remainder of this monograph is based largely on the use of selected monthly data. As subsequent chapters indicate, the use of monthly data highlights a number of significant aspects of recent wage behavior that annual data cannot detect.

III. THE GENERAL RELATIONSHIP BETWEEN UNEMPLOYMENT AND WAGES: 1947-1959

The Monthly and Quarterly Relationship

ONE possible explanation for the loose relationship between unemployment and annual wage changes over the postwar period is that the "true" relationship has somehow been "averaged out" by the use of annual data. Another related possibility is that the annual data failed to show a significant relationship because of the existence of comparatively short time lags (that the annual data could not reflect) between shifts in the level of unemployment and resultant changes in wages. The first part of this chapter will describe the results of research designed to test both of these possibilities.

General Conclusions

The two main conclusions of this research are so clear-cut that they can be summarized here: (1) There is no significant *short-run* relationship between the level of unemployment and the rate of change of wages—that is, we should not expect short-run (monthly, bi-monthly, quarterly) variations in the level of unemployment to produce any predictable change in the rate at which wages increase. (2) There is no evidence of any systematic and significant time lag in the relationship between the level of unemployment and money wage adjustments.

The evidence supporting these conclusions is presented below. The reader who is prepared to accept these strong negative conclusions on "authority" may proceed directly to the second part of the chapter, which deals with the behavior of wages in the various phases of the postwar business cycles.

Unemployment and Wages: 1947-1959

The Relationship Between Unemployment and an
Aggregative Index of Wages and Salaries

A serious shortcoming of the historical comparisons presented in the previous chapter is that they were, of necessity, based on a comparison between aggregative unemployment and the wage behavior of but a small segment of the work-force—namely, average hourly earnings of production workers in manufacturing industries. For the period since January 1947, it is possible to remedy this difficulty by constructing a more comprehensive wage series which will measure monthly changes in the average annual compensation (including supplements) of the entire civilian labor force, and to compare the movement of unemployment with this more inclusive measure of wage and salary behavior as well as with the standard series measuring wages paid manufacturing production workers.[1]

The analysis of the relationship between monthly unemployment and the monthly percentage change in the average compensation of the civilian labor force indicates that—there is no significant relationship at all![2]

In an effort to see if this very weak (non-existent?) relationship between monthly changes in average compensation and the monthly level of unemployment is due to the existence of a time lag between a change in the level of unemployment and the resultant change in average compensation, similar correlations were computed using lags of one month, three months, and six months. The one-month and three-month lags failed to turn up any significant results, while the six-month lag led to a

[1] Appendix B contains the aggregative wage-salary data for each month from Jan. 1947 through Dec. 1958, as well as a full explanation of the sources and methods used in the construction of this series. The monthly unemployment series used throughout the remainder of this study measures unemployment as a percentage of the civilian labor force, and is seasonally adjusted. A complete table of seasonally adjusted unemployment rates, incorporating the recent revision in the seasonal adjustment factors, may be found in the April 1960 issue of the *Survey of Current Business*, p. 22.

[2] $r = -.05$ and the 95% confidence limits for r are $-.22 \leqq r \leqq .13$.

Unemployment and Wages: 1947-1959

weak but positive correlation between the level of unemployment and the rate of change of average annual compensation. Consequently, we are forced to conclude that the lack of a significant relationship between monthly unemployment and the monthly change in average compensation is not the result of time lags. Average compensation simply does not seem sensitive to the monthly level of unemployment.

The relationship between quarterly unemployment and the quarterly rate of change of annual compensation is no closer than the monthly relationship.[1] Consequently, it does not seem possible to attribute the lack of significant correlations in the monthly data to short-run disturbances since the use of quarterly data presumably permits sufficient averaging to eliminate this possibility.

The Relationship Between Unemployment and Average Weekly Earnings in Manufacturing

One possible interpretation of the above results is that average compensation for the entire civilian labor force is too heterogeneous and amorphous a wage concept, and that the inclusion of salaries and other "fixed" labor costs in this concept is responsible for the lack of sensitivity to the level of unemployment. In order to check on this possibility, average weekly earnings of production workers in manufacturing was substituted for average compensation of the civilian labor force as the wage variable in the unemployment-money wage correlation.[2]

The results of this experiment are entirely negative. Again, there is no significant correlation between monthly unemployment and the wage change concept ($r = .06$). Furthermore, the use of bi-monthly unemployment and bi-monthly percent-

[1] In fact, the correlation between quarterly unemployment and quarterly changes in compensation happens to be exactly the same as the correlation between the monthly series—namely, $-.05$.

[2] The wage data for manufacturing production workers are from summary sheets on hours and earnings, kindly supplied by the Bureau of Labor Statistics.

Unemployment and Wages: 1947-1959

age changes in average weekly earnings of manufacturing production workers does not make any significant difference in the correlation.

Consequently, we are forced to the conclusion that it is not merely the inclusion of "fixed" salary elements in the average compensation series that results in the lack of responsiveness of wages to the level of unemployment. The fact that the manufacturing wage series produces the same results suggests the general conclusion that we should not expect *short-run* (monthly, bi-monthly, or quarterly) changes in the level of unemployment to produce any predictable change in the rate of adjustment of money wages.

Postwar Business Cycles and Wage Behavior

The lack of a short-run relationship between wages and unemployment could mean one of two things. First, it could mean simply that there is no important relationship between the level of unemployment and the rate at which money wages rise—regardless of the time intervals covered by the analysis. If this were true, we would be forced to conclude that unemployment and wage adjustments are unrelated, that there are no "terms-of-trade" between them, and that monetary-fiscal policy can pursue the objective of high employment without worrying about the direct effects of such a policy on wage behavior. On the other hand, the lack of a short-run relationship could mean that there still may be a relationship between unemployment and wage behavior but that it takes rather pronounced and permanent variations in unemployment to affect the rate of wage increase. From the standpoint of monetary-fiscal policy, it is obviously very important to know which of these two interpretations is the more nearly correct.

Methodology: The Use of Sub-Periods

To test the relationship between money wage adjustments and unemployment over periods that are longer than a quarter

24

and more homogeneous (in terms of the behavior of unemployment) than a year, it is necessary to divide the postwar period into a number of sub-periods, on the basis of the behavior of unemployment. In fact, it is convenient to work with two distinct sets of sub-periods. The characteristics of these two sets of sub-periods are depicted in Table 3, Table 4, and Chart 2.

One of the things we want to know, of course, is whether the behavior of money wages is affected by recessions. The first set of sub-periods has been designed to answer precisely this question, and to this end 1947-59 has been divided into three sub-periods in which unemployment was above 4.3% each month (recession sub-periods) and three sub-periods in which unemployment was generally below 4.3% (plateau periods of relatively low unemployment).[1] The main characteristics of these six sub-periods that constitute Set I can be read from Table 3 and the bottom part of Chart 2. The three recession sub-periods are, of course, sub-periods I.2 (1949 recession), I.4 (1954 recession), and I.6 (1958 recession). The average level of unemployment in these three recession sub-periods was significantly higher than the average level of unemployment in the three "plateau" periods of relatively low unemployment. It should also be noted that all six of these sub-periods contain roughly the same number of months in which unemployment was increasing as months in which unemployment was decreasing. Consequently, the use of this set of sub-periods enables us to compare wage behavior between periods when unemployment was relatively high and periods when unemployment was relatively low, with the direction of change of unemployment held approximately constant.

[1] The precise figure "4.3%" was not chosen as the cut-off point in determining the sub-periods because of any *a priori* conviction that what we call "recessions" occur when and only when unemployment reaches exactly 4.3% of the labor force. For the purposes of the present study 4.3% is a convenient figure because this unemployment percentage just excludes the period from May 1955 to August 1957 (when unemployment was roughly stable at around 4.2%) from the recession category.

TABLE 3

Set I Sub-Periods:
Recessions vs. Low Unemployment Sub-Periods

Set I Sub-Periods	Length of Sub-Periods (months)	Mean Level of Unemployment (%)	Range of Unemployment (%)	No. of Months that Unemployment Increased, Decreased, Remained Same; Compared to Previous Month
I.1 Jan. 1947-Dec. 1948	24	3.85	3.3-4.5	Inc.: 11 / Dec.: 10 / Same: 2
*I.2 Jan. 1949-Sept. 1950	21	5.84	4.4-7.8	Inc.: 8 / Dec.: 10 / Same: 2
I.3 Oct. 1950-Nov. 1953	38	3.18	2.6-4.3	Inc.: 14 / Dec.: 15 / Same: 8
*I.4 Dec. 1953-Apr. 1955	17	5.32	4.5-6.2	Inc.: 9 / Dec.: 7 / Same: 0
I.5 May 1955-Aug. 1957	28	4.17	3.8-4.5	Inc.: 9 / Dec.: 13 / Same: 5
*I.6 Sept. 1957-May 1959	21	6.17	4.5-7.5	Inc.: 10 / Dec.: 9 / Same: 1

* Periods in which unemployment was above 4.3% each month.

Unemployment and Wages: 1947-1959

TABLE 4

SET II SUB-PERIODS:
CONTRACTION VS. RECOVERY PHASES OF RECESSIONS

Sub-Periods Set II	Length of Sub-Periods (months)	Mean Level of Unemployment (%)	Range of Unemployment (%)	No. of Months that Unemployment Increased, Decreased, Remained Same; Compared to Previous Month
*II.1 Jan. 1949- Oct. 1949	10	5.93	4.4-7.8	Inc.: 7 Dec.: 2 Same: 0
†II.2 Nov. 1949- Sept. 1950	11	5.76	4.5-6.6	Inc.: 1 Dec.: 7 Same: 2
*II.3 Dec. 1953- Aug. 1954	9	5.46	4.5-6.0	Inc.: 7 Dec.: 1 Same: 0
†II.4 Sept. 1954- Apr. 1955	8	5.18	4.2-6.2	Inc.: 1 Dec.: 6 Same: 0
*II.5 Sept. 1957- July 1958	11	6.14	4.5-7.3	Inc.: 8 Dec.: 1 Same: 1
†II.6 Aug. 1958- May 1959	10	6.20	4.9-7.5	Inc.: 1 Dec.: 8 Same: 0

* Periods in which unemployment was above 4.3% and *increasing* steadily (contraction phases of recessions).
† Periods in which unemployment was above 4.3% and *decreasing* steadily (recovery phases of recessions).

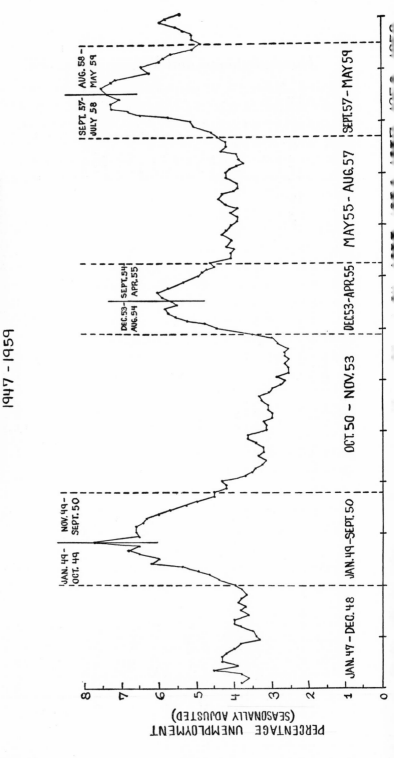

CHART 2
SUB-PERIODS FOR STUDY:
BASED ON
MONTHLY UNEMPLOYMENT RATES (SEASONALLY ADJUSTED)
1947 - 1959

Unemployment and Wages: 1947-1959

We are, however, also interested in knowing whether the behavior of money wages is affected by the direction in which unemployment is changing as well as by the level of unemployment. The second set of sub-periods has been designed to answer this question, and thus each of the three recession sub-periods of Set I has in turn been divided into a sub-period when unemployment was increasing steadily (the contraction phase of the recession) and a sub-period when unemployment was decreasing steadily (the recovery phase of the recession). The main characteristics of these six sub-periods that constitute Set II can be read from Table 4 and the top half of Chart 2. It should be noted that the average level of unemployment is approximately the same in the three sub-periods when unemployment was steadily increasing (II.1, II.3, II.5) as in the three sub-periods when unemployment was steadily decreasing (II.2, II.4, II.6). Consequently, the use of Set II sub-periods enables us to compare wage behavior between periods when unemployment was steadily increasing and periods when unemployment was steadily decreasing, with the average level of unemployment held approximately constant.[1]

Wage Behavior in Recessions and in Periods of Low Unemployment

Let us now compare the behavior of wages in recessions with the behavior of wages in times of low unemployment, using the Set I sub-periods described above. Perhaps the best way to get an over-all impression of the relative change in wages that has occurred when unemployment was relatively low and when unemployment was relatively high is to compare the median

[1] It is because of the desire to examine the effect of both the average level of unemployment and the direction of change of unemployment when the other is held constant that recession months are marked off on the basis of a specific unemployment percentage (4.3%) rather than on the basis of the months in which unemployment was increasing and then decreasing steadily. The use of the specific unemployment percentage is also useful in testing for a trend in the relationship between unemployment and wage behavior (see Chap. IV).

Unemployment and Wages: 1947-1959

wage increase that occurred in the three low unemployment sub-periods with the median wage increase that occurred in the three recession sub-periods.[1] As Table 5 indicates, wages have gone up significantly faster when unemployment was less than 4.3% than when unemployment was steadily above 4.3%. This conclusion holds for both the aggregative wage series measuring changes in compensation of all civilian employees and for average hourly earnings in manufacturing industries. In all manufacturing industries, the median wage increase in low unemployment periods was 6.3%, whereas the median wage increase in the three recessions was 3.9%; hence the median wage increase was 2.4%/annum larger in the low unemployment periods than in the recessions. Or, expressed another way, wages went up more than half again as rapidly in the low unemployment periods than in the recession periods.[2]

The extremely wide distribution of the impact of the recessions on wage behavior is brought out well by an examination of the median wage increases in each of the 20 major 2-digit industries that comprise the manufacturing sector. As Table 5 indicates, the median wage increase in low unemployment periods was greater than the median wage increase in recessions in 18 of the 20 2-digit industries. Only in the case of tobacco and lumber did wages rise faster in recessions than in times of generally low unemployment.[3] Additional evidence of the marked

[1] With the exception of the "wage" figures for all civilian employees described earlier in this chapter, all wage changes referred to are percentage changes in the average hourly earnings paid production workers in manufacturing industries. Wage changes during all sub-periods are expressed at annual rates in order to permit comparisons between sub-periods of unequal duration. The percentage increases in wages that occurred during all sub-periods (Sets I and II) are contained in Appendix C, along with a discussion of sources and methods.

[2] If fringe benefits were included in the wage data, it is likely that the quantitative difference in wage behavior between low unemployment periods and recessions would be reduced somewhat, since many fringes are less flexible than straight wage payments.

[3] A further advantage of disaggregating the manufacturing sector into its 2-digit industry components (in addition to being able to judge the uniformity of wage behavior) is that disaggregation makes it possible to

Unemployment and Wages: 1947-1959

effect of recessions on wage behavior is afforded by the fact that in manufacturing as a whole, as well as in 12 of the 20 2-digit industries, the smallest wage increase that occurred in the three low unemployment periods was larger than the largest wage increase that occurred in the three recession periods.

TABLE 5
A COMPARISON OF WAGE BEHAVIOR
IN RECESSIONS AND IN LOW UNEMPLOYMENT PERIODS

	Median Wage Increase (%) When Unemployment Was		
	(1) Less Than 4.3%	(2) Greater Than 4.3%	(3) (1) — (2)
All Civilian Employees	5.9	4.3	1.6
All Manufacturing	6.3	3.9	2.4
2-Digit Mfg. Industries:			
Ordnance	6.9	4.6	2.3
Food	7.2	3.9	3.3
Tobacco	5.3	8.5	—3.2
Textiles	4.0	2.6	1.4
Apparel	4.0	—0.4	4.4
Lumber	4.4	4.7	—0.3
Furniture	5.9	1.9	4.0
Paper	6.4	3.7	2.7
Printing	5.2	3.8	1.4
Chemicals	6.9	4.3	2.6
Petroleum	6.7	3.1	3.6
Rubber	6.9	4.0	2.9
Leather	4.2	2.3	1.9
Stone, Clay, Glass	5.6	3.6	2.0
Primary Metals	7.8	3.7	4.1
Fabricated Metals	6.1	4.1	2.0
Machinery (Except Electrical)	6.6	4.6	2.0
Electrical Machinery	6.2	3.1	3.1
Transportation Equipment	5.8	4.2	1.6
Instruments	6.1	4.3	1.8

Source: Appendix C.

test (in an admittedly rough fashion) for the statistical significance of the difference in wage behavior between recessions and low unemployment periods. The simple sign test indicates that the difference in wage behavior between recessions and low unemployment periods is significant at the 1% level of significance.

Unemployment and Wages: 1947-1959

On the basis of this evidence we are now able to answer the question posed at the start of this section. The level of unemployment does have a significant effect on wage behavior when we compare relatively long periods in which unemployment was definitely high and definitely low. In recessions, the rate at which money wages increase is reduced relative to the rate at which money wages increase in "good" times.

This does not mean, however, that wages fall during periods of sustained high unemployment—or even that they go up at a slower rate than the long-term rate of productivity increase for the economy as a whole. The median wage increase during the three recessions was greater than 2.5%/year in manufacturing as a whole (where it was 3.9%) as well as in 17 of the 20 industries that make up the manufacturing sector. Only in Apparel was the median wage increase during the three recessions negative (−0.4%).[1]

Wage Behavior in Contraction and Recovery Phases of Recessions

The dampening effect of recessions on wage behavior is by no means the only positive conclusion to emerge from our analysis of 1947-59 sub-periods. Equally striking is the marked effect on wage behavior of the direction in which unemployment is changing. Table 6 indicates that wages go up much less rapidly in the contraction phase of recessions (when unemployment is increasing steadily) than in the recovery phase (when unemployment is decreasing steadily). Not only is the median wage increase for all civilian employees and for manufacturing as a whole much smaller during the three sub-periods when unemployment was increasing, but this same result also holds for 18 of the 20 2-digit manufacturing industries. This time Apparel and Ordnance are the exceptions, and the situation in Ordnance is so heavily determined by the temperature of cold and hot

---

[1] The characteristics of the specific 2-digit industries in which recessions seem to have the most pronounced impact on wage adjustments are analyzed in detail in Chapter V.

Unemployment and Wages: 1947-1959

TABLE 6

A COMPARISON OF WAGE BEHAVIOR
IN CONTRACTION AND RECOVERY PHASES OF RECESSIONS

| | Median Wage Increase (%) When Unemployment Was Greater Than 4.3% and | | |
	(1) Increasing	(2) Decreasing	(3) (1) — (2)
All Civilian Employees	—0.2	7.4	—7.6
All Manufacturing	0.4	5.0	—4.6
2-Digit Mfg. Industries:			
Ordnance	5.0	3.8	1.2
Food	1.1	7.3	—6.2
Tobacco	2.8	10.6	—7.8
Textiles	—0.2	5.5	—5.7
Apparel	0.0	—1.6	1.6
Lumber	3.3	5.0	—1.7
Furniture	0.4	3.4	—3.0
Paper	2.2	4.0	—1.8
Printing	3.1	3.9	—0.8
Chemicals	2.4	4.0	—1.6
Petroleum	1.6	3.9	—2.3
Rubber	2.0	5.3	—3.3
Leather	0.5	3.8	—3.3
Stone, Clay, Glass	2.0	4.6	—2.6
Primary Metals	2.2	6.0	—3.8
Fabricated Metals	1.2	4.7	—3.5
Machinery (Except Electrical)	1.1	6.0	—4.9
Electrical Machinery	0.8	4.4	—3.6
Transportation Equipment	1.4	5.2	—3.8
Instruments	2.5	4.3	—1.8

Source: Appendix C.

wars that its "peculiar" performance should not be given much weight.

Further evidence of the importance of the direction in which the level of unemployment is changing is provided by a separate analysis of each of the three postwar recessions. In the case of both all civilian employees and manufacturing as a whole, wages went up much less rapidly in the contraction phase of *each* recession than in the recovery phase of the same recession.

Unemployment and Wages: 1947-1959

During the 1949 recession, wages in 19 of the 20 2-digit manufacturing industries went up slower when unemployment was increasing than when unemployment was decreasing; during the 1954 recession, 17 of the 20 industries followed this pattern, and during the 1958 recession 16 of the 20 industries experienced smaller wage increases in the contraction phase than in the recovery phase.[1]

Some idea of the magnitude of wage adjustments in contraction and recovery phases of recessions can also be obtained from Table 6. Note the almost negligible wage adjustments that occurred for all civilian employees and for all manufacturing during the contraction phases. Note also that in 15 of the 20 2-digit manufacturing industries the median wage adjustment during the contraction phase of recessions was less than 2.5%/year— and in many cases significantly less than 2.5%. In the recovery phase, on the other hand, wages went up faster than 3%/year in every 2-digit industry but Apparel.

All of this evidence suggests that it is not just a relatively permanent spell of high average levels of unemployment that is capable of reducing the rate at which wages increase (although, as was pointed out earlier, high average levels of unemployment do have a significant braking effect on the size of wage adjustments). The sharpest reductions in the rate at which wages rise occur when unemployment is both above 4.3% *and increasing*. By far the greatest portion of the total dampening effect of postwar recessions on wage behavior has occurred in the contraction phases, when unemployment was rising steadily towards its peak.

[1] The statistical evidence of this paragraph cannot, of course, be read from Table 6, since it contains only the median wage change for all three contractions and all three recoveries. The underlying data can, however, be found in Appendix C as well as in Tables 7-10, contained in the next chapter. Using the sign test, the differences between wage behavior in the contraction and recovery phases of the 1949 and 1954 recessions are significant at the 1% level; the difference in the 1958 recession is significant at the 5% level. The difference between the median wage adjustment in the three contractions taken as a unit and the three recoveries is also significant at the 1% level.

IV. VARIATIONS IN THE RELATIONSHIP BETWEEN UNEMPLOYMENT AND WAGES—AND SOME POSSIBLE EXPLANATIONS

K NOWLEDGE of the "general" or "average" relationship between unemployment conditions and wage adjustments is without question essential to an understanding of the role of wage behavior in recent inflationary episodes. Knowledge of this general relationship is by no means sufficient, however, and must be supplemented by an examination of specific variations that have occurred in this general relationship during the postwar period.

In particular, it is important to find out if there has been any pronounced trend in the magnitude of wage adjustments associated with given unemployment conditions. The wage determination aspect of the inflation problem must certainly be viewed in a more serious light if the same general level of unemployment is producing progressively larger wage increases each succeeding period than if there is no significant time trend in the unemployment-wage relationship. Another important and closely related question is whether variations in the unemployment-wage relationship can be attributed to factors such as changes in manufacturing employment, trends in profit rates, the length of collective bargaining agreements, and the cost-of-living. These two broad sets of questions constitute the subject matter of this chapter.

Economy-Wide Variations in the Unemployment-Wage Relationship

The annual data analyzed in Chapter II suggested that, at given levels of unemployment, wages in the 1947-1959 period as a whole have gone up more rapidly than wages in pre-World

Variations in Recent Wage Behavior

War II years. The question now is: Has this upward trend in the unemployment-wage relationship also occurred *within* the 1947-1959 period?

A Comparison of Wage Behavior in the
Three Low Unemployment Sub-Periods

If we begin by contrasting wage behavior in the three sub-periods when unemployment was both relatively low (below 4.3%) and relatively stable, a rather clear—and, on the face of it, encouraging—picture emerges. Table 7 suggests two unmistakable conclusions. The first conclusion is that the three sub-periods do indeed differ from one another with respect to wage behavior.[1]

The second conclusion is that there is no evidence whatsoever of any secular upward trend in the rate at which wages increase in times of low unemployment. In fact, there is some evidence to suggest the converse. Both average hourly earnings in all manufacturing and average compensation of all civilian employees increased less rapidly in 1955-57 than in either 1947-48 or 1950-53. Whereas the comprehensive index measuring total compensation per civilian employee went up most rapidly in the Korean War period (1950-53), manufacturing wages went up at the fastest rate in 1947-48.[2] Consequently, it would appear that if there is any secular trend in the relation-

[1] The Friedman Two-Way Analysis of Variance test (described in Sidney Siegel, *Nonparametric Statistics for the Behavioral Sciences* [New York: McGraw Hill, 1956], pp. 166-172), applied to the 20 2-digit manufacturing industries, allows us to reject (at the 1% significance level) the null hypothesis that manufacturing wage behavior in all three sub-periods came from the same population.

[2] Wage behavior in the 20 component manufacturing industries is again quite uniform. Wages went up faster in 1947-48 than in 1950-53 in 18 of the 20 2-digit industries; wages also went up faster in 1947-48 than in 1955-57 in 18 of the 20 industries; wages in 1950-53 went up faster than wages in 1955-57 in 12 of the 20 industries and went up at the same rate in 2 of the industries. Using the sign test, the differences in wage behavior between 1947-48 and 1950-53 and between 1947-48 and 1955-57 are significant at the 1% level; the difference in wage behavior between 1950-53 and 1955-57 is not significant at the 5% level.

36

Variations in Recent Wage Behavior

TABLE 7

WAGE BEHAVIOR IN THE LOW UNEMPLOYMENT SUB-PERIODS

	Percentage Increase in Wages in:		
	(I.1) Jan. 1947- Jan. 1949	*(I.3)* Oct. 1950- Dec. 1953	*(I.5)* May 1955- Sept. 1957
All Civilian Employees	5.9	7.9	5.4
All Manufacturing	9.9	6.3	4.8
2-Digit Mfg. Industries:			
Ordnance	6.6	6.9	7.2
Food	9.0	7.2	4.2
Tobacco	5.3	6.3	1.5
Textiles	11.2	1.8	4.0
Apparel	4.0	3.6	5.8
Lumber	8.5	4.2	4.4
Furniture	8.6	5.9	4.5
Paper	11.4	6.2	6.4
Printing	12.5	5.2	3.3
Chemicals	10.9	6.9	5.8
Petroleum	13.9	6.6	6.7
Rubber	7.2	6.9	4.3
Leather	5.7	4.2	4.2
Stone, Clay, Glass	10.1	5.6	5.6
Primary Metals	11.2	7.8	7.5
Fabricated Metals	10.0	6.1	5.7
Machinery (except Electrical)	9.6	6.6	5.2
Electrical Machinery	10.1	6.2	4.8
Transportation Equipment	10.0	5.8	4.5
Instruments	9.7	6.1	6.0

Source: Appendix C.

ship between wages and low levels of unemployment it is in the downward, not the upward, direction. In manufacturing, at any rate, wages went up *less* rapidly in each succeeding period of low unemployment.

However, it would be very unwise to project this trend into the future and to infer that in future periods of relatively low unemployment wages will rise less rapidly than they did in the 1955-57 period. First of all, it is necessary to remember that war-related phenomena were largely responsible for the high rate of wage increase during 1947-48 and during 1950-53. Also,

Variations in Recent Wage Behavior

average unemployment was somewhat higher in 1955-57 than in either of the two earlier periods of relatively low unemployment. Consequently, wages in 1955-57 may have gone up less rapidly because of the absence of war-related demand pressures and because of the generally higher level of unemployment. The special characteristics of each of the three low unemployment periods prevents us from predicting with any degree of confidence whether future low unemployment periods will produce smaller or larger wage increases than the 1955-57 period.

A Comparison of Wage Behavior in the Three Postwar Recessions

Fortunately for purposes of analysis, the three recession subperiods are sufficiently similar in salient respects to permit at least general comparisons of wage behavior. And, the most general conclusion that can be drawn is that there has not been any pronounced secular trend in wage behavior in either direction over the course of all three recessions. While we can be quite confident that the three recessions do differ from one another with respect to the rate at which wages increased, this lack of uniformity seems to be due mainly to the fact that wage behavior in the middle (1954) recession differed significantly from wage behavior in the 1949 and 1958 recessions.[1]

It is quite clear from Table 8 that wages went up less rapidly in the 1954 recession than in either the 1949 or the 1958 recession. Over the course of the 1954 recession, the average aggregate compensation of all civilian employees rose 3.3%/year, while this same wage statistic rose at the rate of 5.5%/year and 4.3%/year in the 1949 and 1958 recessions, respectively. Aver-

---

[1] For purposes of expositional convenience, the three recessions are identified by the years in which peak unemployment occurred. The precise periods included within each recession for the purposes of this analysis are listed in Table 3. Application of the Friedman test to wage behavior in the 20 2-digit manufacturing industries allows us to reject, at the 1% level of significance, the null hypothesis that wage adjustments in all three recessions came from the same population.

Variations in Recent Wage Behavior

age hourly earnings in all manufacturing rose only 2.8%/year in the 1954 recession, as against 3.9%/year and 4.4%/year in the other two recessions. And, this same pattern of wage behavior occurred with remarkable uniformity among the 2-digit manufacturing industries.

Of particular significance is the fact that wages went up at the slowest rate during the 1954 recession *in spite of the fact that this was by far the mildest of the three postwar recessions.* (See Table 3 and Chart 2, in Chapter III.)

A comparison of the 1949 and 1958 recessions produces far more ambiguous results. For all civilian employees, wages and salaries went up at a *slower* rate in the 1958 recession than in the 1949 recession (4.3%/year versus 5.5%/year). For all manufacturing production workers, however, wages went up *faster* in the 1958 recession than in the 1949 recession (4.4%/year versus 3.9%/year). To complicate things still further, wage behavior in a majority of the 2-digit industries comprising the manufacturing sector contradicts the behavior of wages in manufacturing as a whole. In 13 of the 20 manufacturing industries, wages went up at a *slower* rate in the 1958 recession than in the 1949 recession.[1] The only safe conclusion to draw from this morass of conflicting evidence is that there is no clear evidence of any pronounced and consistent difference in overall wage behavior between the 1949 and 1958 recessions.

More generally, there is no evidence of any pronounced secular trend covering wage behavior in all three postwar recessions. While wages went up faster in the 1958 recession than in the 1954 recession, wages also went up faster in the 1949 recession than in the 1954 recession; and it is just difficult to say whether wages went up faster or slower over the course of the

---

[1] This difference between the behavior of the aggregative index for all manufacturing and the behavior of the components is due to a highly complicated weighting problem involved in computing the percentage changes in wages for the component industries and for the manufacturing aggregate. For present purposes, the importance of this phenomenon is that it underlines the lack of a uniform pattern of wage behavior.

Variations in Recent Wage Behavior

TABLE 8

WAGE BEHAVIOR IN THE RECESSION SUB-PERIODS

	Percentage Increase in Wages in:		
	(I.2) Jan. 1949- Oct. 1950	(I.4) Dec. 1953- May 1955	(I.6) Sept. 1957- June 1959
All Civilian Employees	5.5	3.3	4.3
All Manufacturing	3.9	2.8	4.4
2-Digit Mfg. Industries:			
Ordnance	6.8	3.7	4.6
Food	3.4	3.9	5.4
Tobacco	3.7	8.5	11.0
Textiles	4.7	0.5	2.6
Apparel	−0.1	−1.6	−0.4
Lumber	8.4	3.5	4.7
Furniture	4.4	1.3	1.9
Paper	4.4	3.7	3.3
Printing	5.0	3.1	3.8
Chemicals	5.4	4.2	4.3
Petroleum	2.9	3.1	3.1
Rubber	3.1	5.5	4.0
Leather	4.1	1.6	2.3
Stone, Clay, Glass	5.3	3.6	3.6
Primary Metals	2.6	3.7	6.0
Fabricated Metals	4.9	3.0	4.1
Machinery (except Electrical)	4.9	2.5	4.6
Electrical Machinery	3.1	2.3	4.1
Transportation Equipment	4.2	3.7	4.9
Instruments	5.8	1.9	4.3

Source: Appendix C.

1958 recession compared with the 1949 recession. The slower rate of wage increase in the 1954 recession seems to contradict any notion of an inexorable and irreversible upward trend in the magnitude of wage adjustments over successive recessions.

A Comparison of Wage Behavior in the Contraction and Recovery Phases of the Recessions

Additional light is thrown on the differences in recession wage behavior by sub-dividing each recession into two parts and looking at the contraction and recovery phases separately.

Variations in Recent Wage Behavior

If we compare only the contraction phases of the three recessions (Table 9), the hypothesis that wages have been in-

TABLE 9

WAGE BEHAVIOR IN THE CONTRACTION SUB-PERIODS

	Percentage Increase in Wages in:		
	(II.1) Jan. 1949- Nov. 1949	(II.3) Dec. 1953- Sept. 1954	(II.5) Sept. 1957- Aug. 1958
All Civilian Employees	−3.4	−0.2	2.1
All Manufacturing	−1.1	0.4	2.6
2-Digit Mfg. Industries:			
Ordnance	5.8	3.1	5.0
Food	1.1	0.0	3.4
Tobacco	2.8	−0.6	10.9
Textiles	−0.2	−0.5	0.0
Apparel	−8.9	0.0	0.8
Lumber	5.5	3.3	4.1
Furniture	0.4	0.4	0.7
Paper	1.9	2.2	2.6
Printing	5.9	1.4	3.1
Chemicals	2.3	2.4	4.4
Petroleum	1.6	2.0	0.0
Rubber	0.6	2.0	4.8
Leather	0.5	0.0	0.7
Stone, Clay, Glass	2.0	1.7	2.6
Primary Metals	−1.1	2.2	5.6
Fabricated Metals	−0.1	1.2	3.5
Machinery (except Electrical)	1.1	1.1	2.8
Electrical Machinery	−0.4	0.8	3.7
Transportation Equipment	0.0	1.4	4.5
Instruments	2.5	1.2	4.1

Source: Appendix C.

creasing ever more rapidly in successive recessions receives considerably more support than it did when the recessions as a whole were compared. During the contraction phase of the 1949 recession, the average compensation of civilian employees and the average hourly earnings of manufacturing production workers *fell;* during the contraction phase of the 1954 recession, there was almost *no perceptible change* in the earnings of

41

Variations in Recent Wage Behavior

either all civilian employees or manufacturing production work-ers; during the contraction phase of the 1958 recession, average compensation of civilian employees and manufacturing wages both *rose* more than 2%/year.

A comparison of the recovery phases of the three recessions (Table 10) reveals almost exactly the opposite pattern. The re-

TABLE 10

WAGE BEHAVIOR IN RECOVERY SUB-PERIODS

	Percentage Increase in Wages in:		
	(II.2) Nov. 1949- Oct. 1950	(II.4) Sept. 1954- May 1955	(II.6) Aug. 1958- June 1959
All Civilian Employees	13.9	7.4	6.6
All Manufacturing	8.5	5.0	6.2
2-Digit Mfg. Industries:			
Ordnance	7.4	1.5	3.8
Food	5.6	8.2	7.3
Tobacco	4.5	19.3	10.6
Textiles	9.2	2.2	5.5
Apparel	8.6	—3.3	—1.6
Lumber	10.9	0.9	5.0
Furniture	8.0	1.9	3.4
Paper	6.5	3.5	4.0
Printing	3.9	3.9	4.4
Chemicals	8.0	3.9	4.0
Petroleum	3.9	2.5	6.6
Rubber	5.3	7.6	3.0
Leather	7.3	3.3	3.8
Stone, Clay, Glass	8.2	4.2	4.6
Primary Metals	6.0	3.5	6.2
Fabricated Metals	9.4	3.9	4.7
Machinery (except Electrical)	8.3	3.0	6.0
Electrical Machinery	6.3	3.3	4.4
Transportation Equipment	8.0	4.9	5.2
Instruments	8.6	1.6	4.3

Source: Appendix C.

covery phase of the 1949 recession witnessed a much more rapid increase in average compensation of civilian employees and in manufacturing wages than the recovery phases of the two subsequent recessions. The average compensation of all civilian employees also increased more rapidly in the recovery phase of the 1954 recession than in the recovery phase of the 1958 recession. This impression of a steady downward trend in the rate of wage increase accompanying the recovery phases of recessions is interrupted, however, by the fact that manufacturing hourly earnings rose less rapidly in the recovery phase of the 1954 recession than in the recovery phase of the 1958 recession.

If we now combine this analysis of contraction and recovery phases with our earlier discussion of wage behavior over the recession as a whole, a somewhat more useful comparison of wage behavior in the three recessions is possible. (Chart 3 portrays this combined picture, with the slopes of the three straight lines drawn for each recession depicting the rate at which all manufacturing wages changed over the course of the recession as a whole and over both the contraction and expansion phases considered separately.) There is no need to re-compare the 1954 recession with the other two recessions since the conclusion of the preceding section still holds: wages went up less rapidly in the 1954 recession as a whole than in either of the other two recession periods.

The comparison between wage behavior in the 1949 and 1958 recessions is, however, worth reconsidering. Whereas we concluded earlier that is was hard to tell which of these recessions witnessed the largest overall wage increase, it is now clear that this stalemate was the product of two markedly different trends. Wages went up much *faster* in the contraction phase of the 1958 recession than in the contraction phase of the 1949 recession, but wages went up much *slower* in the recovery phase of the 1958 recession than in the recovery phase of the 1949 recession.

At this point, a piece of military-economic history becomes highly relevant. The Korean War broke out on June 25, 1950—

Variations in Recent Wage Behavior

in the midst of the recovery from the trough of the 1949 recession and approximately four months before unemployment fell below 4.3%. The month-by-month plot of manufacturing wages in Chart 3 shows clearly that the Korean mobilization accentuated the rate of wage increase during the latter part of the recovery phase of the 1949 recession. Not only did the normal expectational effects influence wage and price behavior, but the prospects of war-time wage and price controls also encouraged unions and companies to raise wages very quickly. Consequently, a significant part of the relatively rapid wage increase that occurred in the recovery phase of the 1949 recession must be attributed to the Korean situation and cannot be interpreted as the result of "normal" economic forces.

When some allowance is made for the influence of the Korean War, the earlier conclusion that there was no noticeable difference in the unemployment-wage relationship between the 1949 and 1958 recessions becomes suspect. If it were possible to subtract that portion of the overall rate of wage increase in the 1949 recession attributable to the expectational effects of the Korean War, it seems quite likely that the remaining, "adjusted" rate of wage increase would be noticeably smaller than the rate of wage increase in the 1958 recession.

In short, there are grounds for thinking that the "normal," or "non-war-induced" rate of wage increase was larger in the 1958 recession than in either of the two previous recessions. We may be experiencing at least a slight upward trend in the relationship between wages and recession levels of unemployment after all.

Some Possible Explanations

How are these variations in the unemployment-wage relationship between periods to be explained? The most obvious possibility is that broad changes in economic and institutional factors other than unemployment conditions are at work and

Variations in Recent Wage Behavior

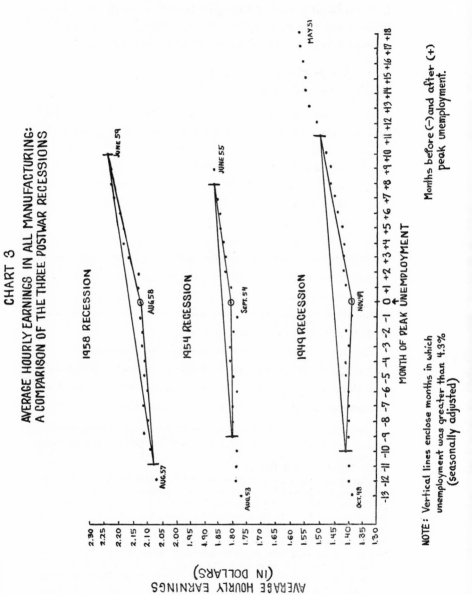

CHART 3

AVERAGE HOURLY EARNINGS IN ALL MANUFACTURING:
A COMPARISON OF THE THREE POSTWAR RECESSIONS

1958 RECESSION

1954 RECESSION

1949 RECESSION

AVERAGE HOURLY EARNINGS
(IN DOLLARS)

MONTH OF PEAK UNEMPLOYMENT

Months before (–) and after (+) peak unemployment.

NOTE: Vertical lines enclose months in which unemployment was greater than 4.3% (seasonally adjusted)

Variations in Recent Wage Behavior

that to obtain a more meaningful picture of wage behavior it is necessary to consider these factors along with the level of unemployment and the direction in which it is changing.

The Behavior of Manufacturing Employment and Profits

Two factors that might be expected to exert an independent influence on wage behavior are changes in manufacturing employment and differences in average profit levels. We would expect that, at given levels of unemployment, manufacturing wages would go up faster the more rapidly manufacturing employment was increasing (or the slower it was decreasing) and the higher the average level of profits.[1]

To test the importance of these two factors, an attempt was made to explain differences in the rate of wage increase among recession sub-periods, and among the contraction phases of the recessions, on the basis of differences in the rate of change of manufacturing employment and differences in the level and rate of change of manufacturing profits.[2]

This attempt was not very successful. For instance, we know that wages went up faster in the 1958 recession than in the 1954 recession. And yet, none of the relevant measures of variations in manufacturing employment suggest that the 1958 recession

[1] For a discussion of the reasoning behind these expected relationships, see my *The Wage-Price Issue: A Theoretical Analysis* (Princeton, N. J.: Princeton University Press, 1960), pp. 92-112 and pp. 113-124, as well as the literature cited therein.

[2] No effort was made to explain differences among the three low unemployment sub-periods in terms of manufacturing employment and profits since war-related phenomena loom so large in any explanation of wage behavior in 1947-48 and 1950-53. From here on all analysis will be restricted to the manufacturing sector, since the necessary data are simply not available for "all civilian employees." The manufacturing employment data used here measure seasonally adjusted monthly totals of production workers in manufacturing establishments; the manufacturing profits data measure the average rate of return on stockholders' equity after taxes. The employment and profits data for all manufacturing and for the component 2-digit industries, as well as an explanation of sources and methods, are contained in Appendix C.

Variations in Recent Wage Behavior

was milder in this respect than its 1954 counterpart.[1] Furthermore, average profits levels were lower and declined more rapidly in the 1958 recession than in the 1954 recession. Profits were also lower and employment declined more rapidly in the contraction phase of the 1958 recession than in the contraction phase of the 1949 recession—and yet wages declined in the contraction phase of the 1949 recession and rose more than 2%/year in the 1958 contraction phase. The general level of profits and the rate of change of manufacturing employment are more successful in explaining why wages rose at a faster rate in the 1949 recession as a whole than in the 1954 recession. However, it is difficult to attach much importance to this single success.

It looks as if broad trends in after-tax profits and employment cannot, by themselves, be depended on to help explain variations in the unemployment-wage relationship over time. The next two factors to be considered—the length of collective bargaining agreements and changes in the cost of living—offer somewhat more promise.

Significance of Long-Term Collective Bargaining Agreements

The great importance of long-term contracts in the 1958 recession has been suggested as an alternative explanation of why wages rose faster in this recession, and the available data cannot be used to disprove this hypothesis. The popularity of long-term contracts containing provisions for deferred increases reached a peak immediately preceding the 1958 recession, as this brief history of the evolution of long-term contracts indicates:

[1] The trend in manufacturing employment between the beginning and the end of each recession was the same in 1958 and in 1954. The number of production workers employed in all manufacturing at the end of both recessions was 0.8% lower (at an annual rate) than at the start of the recessions. To measure how far employment declined below this trend-line when unemployment was at its peak, an index of employment flexibility was constructed. This index shows that manufacturing employment dropped much more sharply at the peak of the 1958 recession than at the peak of the 1954 recession.

47

Variations in Recent Wage Behavior

Contracts effective for periods of more than a year (frequently 2, 3, or even 5 years) and providing for deferred or "installment" wage increases are not a new development, although they currently [January 1957] cover more than twice as many workers as in 1951—the period of previous peak coverage of such arrangements. (Footnote: By early 1951, the number of workers covered by provisions for deferred wage increases rose to about 2 million. Most of these workers were in the automobile, farm equipment, and related industries, utilities, construction, and transportation.) In 1950, anticipation of wage controls during the Korean conflict gave impetus to long-term arrangements providing "annual improvement," "productivity," or deferred wage increases. Even then, however, the vast majority of contracts continued to follow the traditional pattern of negotiating with respect to wages for a single year or of providing for annual wage reopenings.

In 1955, spurred by the renewal of existing long-term agreements (notably in automobiles and related industries) for 3-year periods and the new 5-year agreements negotiated by the General Electric Co., labor-management interest was revived in such arrangements. The spread of deferred increases became even more rapid during 1956 with the adoption in that year of provisions for deferred increases and periodic cost-of-living adjustments in major agreements in steel, meat-packing, and railroads, as well as some other situations. Altogether, more than 350 contracts stipulating wage increases in 1957 for about 3 million workers were negotiated in 1956—the peak year for conclusion of such agreements whether measured by number of situations or number of workers covered.

When account is taken of all major contracts in effect at the end of 1956 that specify wage rate increases in 1957, the number rises to more than 550 contracts covering about 5 million workers.[1]

More recent studies by the Bureau of Labor Statistics demonstrate that this 1957 "peak" in the popularity of long-term agreements was not really a peak at all, but rather the beginning of a plateau that has extended right up to the present time. The appeal of the long-term agreement was by no means destroyed by the 1958 recession, and the vast majority of long-term agreements that expired during that episode were renewed with new provisions for deferred increases.[2] A study of major agreements

[1] *Monthly Labor Review,* January 1957, p. 50. For lists of companies operating under long-term contracts in specific years prior to 1957, see U. S. Department of Labor, Bureau of Labor Statistics, Report No. 102, Report No. 75, and Bulletin No. 17.
[2] *Monthly Labor Review*, December 1958, p. 1362.

Variations in Recent Wage Behavior

in effect January 1, 1959, revealed that 85% of the 283 agreements with fixed terms were negotiated for periods of two years or longer, and the major concentration was at the three year mark.[1] It looks very much as if long-term agreements are going to cover a significant proportion of the manufacturing work-force for some time to come.

The direct effect of long-term agreements on wages in a given year depends, in the first instance, on the size of the deferred increases written into the contract and on the number of workers who are scheduled to obtain deferred increases in the year in question. In 1957, approximately five million workers received deferred increases, and the magnitude of the increases ranged up to 9-10¢/hour in basic steel. In 1958, approximately four million workers received deferred wage increases, with the amount of the increase ranging up to 8-9¢/hour in basic steel, electrical equipment, and aluminum.[2]

While it would certainly be a mistake to assume that in the absence of long-term contracts no wage adjustments at all would have occurred in 1957 and 1958, it would be equally unwise to assume that the deferred increases—negotiated, it must be remembered, in relatively prosperous times—were not larger than the wage increases that could have been obtained by regular negotiations. And, it is not just the workers directly affected who benefit from these deferred increases. By means of labor market pressures, the internal politics of union wage policy formulation, and the process of invidious comparison, automatic wage increases tend to spread (to some unknown extent) to other workers. Consequently, the proposition that the popularity of long-term contracts increased the speed with which manufacturing wages rose during the 1958 recession is

[1] *Monthly Labor Review*, December 1958, pp. 1349-1361. A similar study of agreements in effect January 1, 1960 (*Monthly Labor Review*, December 1959, pp. 1312-1323) suggests essentially the same situation.
[2] The data in this paragraph have been taken from the *Monthly Labor Review*, January 1957, p. 51; and December 1957, pp. 1464-1466.

Variations in Recent Wage Behavior

consistent with the available evidence and seems plausible on *a priori* grounds as well.

However, it is highly important to recognize that this does not mean that long-term contracts per se will always exert as much upward pressure on wages as they did in 1958. As the experience in the 1958 recession illustrates, the effect of long-term agreements on the magnitude of wage increases depends to a considerable extent on the timing of major long-term agreements vis-à-vis recessions. In the case of the 1958 recession, it happened that a sizeable cluster of important long-term agreements were negotiated in 1955 and 1956, when economic conditions were quite favorable, and that these long-term agreements then continued to produce wage increases throughout the 1957-59 recession. There is, however, no inexorable law to suggest that the next recession will follow on the heels of a concentrated bunching of new long-term agreements negotiated in prosperous times.

At the same time we should recognize that the institution of the long-term contract probably does complicate the job of monetary-fiscal policy by both reducing the speed with which changes in aggregate demand can be expected to influence wages and by raising the long-term rate at which money wages are likely to rise. The reason why long-term contracts (almost by definition) reduce the flexibility of wages in response to sudden changes in levels of aggregate demand and unemployment is obvious and need not be spelled out.

The assertion that long-term contracts also increase the long-term rate at which money wages rise is less clear-cut and requires brief elaboration. This assertion is based on three considerations. First, the timing of negotiations with respect to recessions is not purely a matter of chance, and there are reasons for thinking that unions have somewhat more influence than companies in determining when negotiations actually take place. The success of the U.A.W. in reopening an apparently closed long-term contract in the Korean War period (on the

Variations in Recent Wage Behavior

basis of Reuther's "living document" interpretation of the contract) and the success of the U.A.W. in delaying the 1958 negotiations from the spring to the fall can be cited as examples of the way an imaginative union can affect the timing of negotiations to suit its own purposes.

In the second place, there are reasons for thinking that the per se advantages of a longer agreement may be greater to a company than to a union and that therefore the company may be willing to pay something extra for the assurance of an uninterrupted period of production. It is particularly likely that a company enjoying some degree of protection from price competition in the product market will prefer to buy a period of guaranteed peace by granting a somewhat larger increase in money wages (and then attempting to recoup a portion of the higher labor costs via product price adjustments) than to gamble on the frequent occurrence of strikes. The industrial customers of such companies may well be more willing to pay slightly higher prices than to run the risk of having sources of supply cut off by industrial strife.

Finally, it is important to remember that in the United States all collective bargaining contracts do not expire at the same time. In any recession there are bound to be some long-term agreements that will provide deferred increases, and since the mechanism of invidious comparison seems to work mainly in one direction—that is, we compare our wage situation with people doing better, not with people doing worse—these deferred increases will exert upward pressure on other wage settlements.

The Cost-of-Living and Wage Behavior

Another possible explanation for the more rapid increase in manufacturing wages during the 1958 recession is inflation itself. And, as in the case of the long-term contract hypothesis, this possible explanation cannot be contradicted by the avail-

Variations in Recent Wage Behavior

able data. For inflation to influence wage behavior, two conditions must, of course, be met: (1) prices must rise; and (2) wages must, in some way, respond to the higher prices.

There is no question but that prices went up faster in the 1958 recession than in either the 1954 or 1949 recessions. Between September 1957 and June 1959 (the precise period that we have loosely been calling the "1958" recession), the Consumer Price Index (CPI) rose at an annual rate of 1.6%. In the 1954 recession, the CPI fell at the rate of −0.4%/year and in the 1949 recession, the CPI rose 1.3%/year. (However, most of the increase in prices that occurred during the 1949 recession came at the end of the recession in response to the Korean emergency.)[1]

There is also no question but that mechanisms linking wages to prices existed in the 1958 recession. Formal escalator clauses are, of course, the most visible and obvious mechanism of this type—and, at the end of 1957, escalator provisions covered more workers than at any previous time. By December 1957, escalators covered 4 million workers under union agreements and 300,000 unorganized workers (mainly clerical employees). The previous peak was in September 1952, when 3.5 million workers were covered by escalation.[2] Between September 1952 and the end of 1955, however, the number of organized workers covered by some type of cost-of-living clause had fallen to 1.7 million. It was in 1956 that escalators were re-instituted in large numbers. There has not been any noticeable trend either toward or away from cost-of-living escalators since the 1958 recession, but there have been some changes in the type of cost-of-living clauses written. The most striking development has been the adoption in some contracts of an upper limit on

[1] These price data have been taken from U. S. Department of Labor, Bureau of Labor Statistics, Bulletin No. 1256, pp. 40-42.

[2] It was the Korean War that gave the first big impetus to the escalator arrangement. Three months before the start of the Korean War, the B.L.S. estimated that only about 800,000 workers were covered by escalators. See *Monthly Labor Review*, February 1953, pp. 126-129.

Variations in Recent Wage Behavior

the size of escalator increases that can occur during the contract period.[1]

Because of the increases in the CPI that occurred, cost-of-living increases were a significant supplement to regular pay raises in 1958, and in some cases approximately equaled increases in basic rates. Steelworkers received 8 or 9 cents/hour in deferred increases and 9 cents in cost-of-living adjustments; most meat-packing workers also did better via cost-of-living adjustments than via deferred increases.[2]

Consequently, it would be very difficult to deny the contention that escalator arrangements had something to do with the larger wage increases that occurred in the 1958 recession. Just how *much* of an effect inflation itself had on wage behavior is, however, extremely hard to say. For one thing, it is important to recognize that unions do not get escalator clauses for nothing and that therefore the amount of cost-of-living wage adjustments cannot be regarded as a net addition to the wage adjustment that would have occurred without an escalator clause. It is significant to note that: "Escalator provisions tend to be more common in those contracts that provide for the smallest cents-per-hour deferred increases. Such provisions are rare in the construction trades, where the most common deferred increases exceed 15 cents an hour."[3]

On the other side of the ledger, we must not make the mistake of assuming that formal escalators constitute the only means whereby price changes can affect wages. The movement of consumer prices is always an important consideration in the negotiation of new contracts, and history shows that even before the days of strong industrial unions wages tended to rise when prices went up rapidly.

[1] See *Monthly Labor Review*, December 1959, p. 1328. Other issues of the *Monthly Labor Review* that have provided data for this paragraph are: December 1957, pp. 1466-1467; January 1957, p. 52; March 1955, pp. 315-318; and February 1953, pp. 126-129.

[2] *Monthly Labor Review*, December 1958, p. 1365.

[3] *Monthly Labor Review*, December 1959, p. 1328.

Variations in Recent Wage Behavior

The final, over-riding difficulty in determining the magnitude of the effect of inflation on wages is, of course, that wage behavior also affects prices. The problem of disentangling cause and effect in a precise way is, in all likelihood, insurmountable. The behavior of wages and prices over the 1957-59 period is compatible with two broad hypotheses: (1) wages—for whatever reason—went up faster than in previous recessions and pushed prices up faster too; (2) prices—for whatever reason—went up faster than in previous recessions and pulled wages along behind them.

While a more detailed analysis of this nexus than is appropriate to the scope of the present study might yield some helpful results, the difficulties involved in distinguishing the effects of prices on wages from the effects of wages on prices warn against expecting a precise determination of the relative validity of these two competing hypotheses. (They are not, of course, mutually exclusive.) All we can conclude at this time is that the sensitivity of wages to prices accounts for at least a part of the larger wage increases in the 1958 recession and that the larger wage increases in turn account for a part of the more rapid rise in the price level. Unfortunately, the crucial questions of "how much" have not as yet been answered.

V. INTER-INDUSTRY VARIATIONS IN THE UNEMPLOYMENT-WAGE RELATIONSHIP

WHILE variations in wage behavior among industries have been noted on occasion in previous chapters, no effort has yet been made to account for these differences in terms of such industry characteristics as unionization, industrial concentration, and profitability. This omission has been deliberate. Too often discussions of wage behavior concentrate on inter-industry differences to such an extent that pronounced similarities in wage behavior between industries pass unnoticed. The data presented in Chapters III and IV of this study show clearly that nationwide unemployment conditions have a generally similar effect on wages in almost all manufacturing industries; furthermore, variations in wage behavior over time (when unemployment conditions are held roughly constant) also tend to be remarkably uniform among industries. The existence of this highly significant general pattern in the relationship between unemployment and wage behavior must not be obscured by undue emphasis on inter-industry differences in wage behavior.

It is, of course, also possible to go too far to the other extreme. Certainly no study of wage behavior in the context of the postwar inflation controversy would be complete without a fairly careful analysis of inter-industry variations in wage behavior, and it is to this task that the present chapter is addressed.

This analysis of inter-industry wage behavior within a given time period is designed to serve three purposes. First, it permits a direct examination of the role played in the wage determination process by two factors not heretofore considered in this study: industrial concentration and the degree of unionization. Second, it permits an examination of the effect on wage behavior of inter-industry differences in profitability and employment trends. Finally, this analysis of inter-industry variations in wage behavior within each of the sub-periods studied earlier holds out the possibility that new light will be shed on some of the trends in overall wage behavior between sub-periods that were described—but not satisfactorily explained—in the previous chapter.

Framework and Methods

Because certain of the relationships discussed in this chapter are shrouded with emotion and charged with controversy, and because the data presented in this chapter are (for various statistical and other reasons) easily misinterpreted, it is necessary at the outset to comment briefly on the design of this inter-industry analysis, on the special characteristics of the data used, and on the statistical techniques employed.

Four variables will be used in an attempt to explain inter-industry differences in wage behavior within each sub-period. These four explanatory variables, chosen on the basis of *a priori* theoretical considerations, are: percentage changes in production worker employment; the average rate of return on stockholders' equity after taxes; the degree of industrial concentration; and the degree of union strength.

The percentage change in production worker employment has been chosen to serve as a very crude index of differential trends in the demand for labor. In an economy characterized by imperfect mobility of labor, we expect wages to go up most rapidly (for relatively short periods, at least) in industries that experience the greatest increase in employment. It will be particularly interesting to see if the employment variable is more closely related to wages when unemployment is generally low than when recessions are underway.[1]

---

[1] Measured changes in both wages and employment represent, of course, the *ex post* results of economic activity. Consequently, we cannot be certain to what extent the measured changes in wages and employment are the result of shifts in the demand schedule for labor coupled

Inter-Industry Wage Behavior

The average level of profits has been chosen as an explanatory variable because of the numerous theoretical and empirical studies that have suggested that high-profit firms are more likely to be liberal with wage increases than low-profit firms. Another reason for including both employment and profit variables is that we need to investigate the inter-relationship between these factors and the degree of industrial concentration and union strength that prevail in various industries.[1]

The reasons for including industrial concentration and unionization are obvious. The effect of both unions and industrial concentration on wages has been hotly debated for quite some time, and there are certainly *a priori* reasons for thinking that the existence of "market power" in both labor and product markets is likely to lead to a greater downward rigidity of wages in time of depression and to a more rapid rate of wage increase in prosperous times. While a comparison of wage behavior between strongly and weakly unionized (and/or concentrated) industries cannot always provide conclusive results because of the tendency for wage adjustments in one industry to affect wages in another industry, such comparisons can, if made carefully, be highly suggestive.

---

with movements along some facsimile of a supply schedule or to what extent the wage and employment changes are the result of shifts in supply conditions and attendant movements along the demand schedule. The interdependence between demand and cost schedules in most manufacturing industries complicates things still more. While this study does not purport to have "solved" this identification problem, the nature of the sub-periods under investigation here provides at least some relief from this general difficulty. Since the sub-periods are marked off by variations in the behavior of unemployment, we have at least a rather strong hint of the sub-periods in which the demand for labor shifted rapidly up or rapidly down. Furthermore, when employment in a given industry increases in spite of an increase in relative wages, we can be reasonably sure that the demand curve for labor in this industry has shifted significantly to the right.

[1] Unfortunately, the wage-profit relationship is subject to the same difficulties as the wage-employment relationship. Not only may profits affect wages, but wages also affect profits. The same general comments made in the last footnote apply here as well.

Inter-Industry Wage Behavior

The problems involved in measuring employment and profits have been mentioned earlier and are discussed in Appendix C. Here it is sufficient to point out that the production worker employment data are seasonally adjusted and that the profit data (which actually measure the average rate of return on stockholders' equity after taxes) have been compiled so as to avoid distortions caused by seasonal variations.[1]

The degree of competition in the product market is measured by the familiar "concentration ratio," which tells us what proportion of the total output (or, in some cases, value added) of an industry is produced by the four largest firms. The concentration ratios used here, as well as a discussion of sources and methods, can be found in Appendix D. In brief, the concentration ratios for each 2-digit manufacturing industry have been calculated by simply averaging the concentration ratios prevailing in 1954 in the 4-digit industries comprising each 2-digit classification. Indices of this sort suffer, of course, from numerous difficulties. In particular, concentration ratios may overstate the actual degree of "monopoly" in an industry that is subject to serious competition from substitute products produced by another industry; on the other hand, concentration ratios may understate the true degree of control over price in industries where the market is primarily local or regional in scope. Nonetheless, concentration ratios do provide at least a general idea of which industries are nearest the "competitive pole," and which industries are nearest the "monopoly pole."

Measuring unionization is no easier than measuring industrial concentration. Fortunately, however, the Bureau of Labor Statistics has recently published data showing the proportion of production workers, in each 2-digit manufacturing industry, that worked (in 1958) in establishments where collective bar-

[1] Because of the lack of data with respect to profits and industrial concentration, it has been necessary to exclude the Ordnance industry from the analysis of this chapter. Consequently, 19 (instead of 20) 2-digit manufacturing industries are included in the following inter-industry comparisons.

Inter-Industry Wage Behavior

gaining agreements cover the majority of the work-force.[1] Although this type of data cannot take account of such considerations as the "independence" of various unions and the "aggressiveness" of various union leaders, the ratios do provide the best index of union strength that is available today.

To analyze the relationships between wage behavior and these four explanatory variables, simple, partial, and multiple correlation techniques have been used. The simple correlation coefficients are used to provide a general idea of the "gross" relationship between wages and each of the explanatory variables. The partial correlation coefficients are used to determine the relationship between wage changes and each of the explanatory variables when the other wage-determining variables are held constant. The multiple correlation coefficients are used to determine the relationship between the rate at which wages in various industries increase and combinations of the four explanatory variables. The potential pitfalls in interpreting each of these coefficients will be noted at appropriate points.

The Significance of Individual
Wage-Determining Variables

To gain some measure of perspective, it is convenient to begin with a general comparison of the relation between wage adjustments and each of the four explanatory variables. More specific comments on the wage-determining significance of employment trends, profits, industrial concentration, and unionization will follow this general commentary.

A General Commentary

The simple correlation coefficients presented in Table 11 provide an initial impression of the strength and direction of

[1] H. M. Douty, "Collective Bargaining Coverage in Factory Employment, 1958," *Monthly Labor Review*, April 1960, pp. 345-349. A tabular summary of this measure of union strength by industry is contained in Appendix *D*.

Inter-Industry Wage Behavior

the relationship between wage adjustments and each of the four explanatory variables.

The most general conclusion to be drawn from this table is that, in most cases, the four explanatory variables chosen for study do seem to affect the pattern of wage behavior between industries in the direction suggested by *a priori* speculation. This conclusion is based on the preponderance of positive correlations and on the fact that out of the 24 correlation coefficients contained in Table 11, 9 are sufficiently large to be statistically significant at the 5% level of significance (that is, we can be 95% certain that the "true" correlation coefficient does differ from 0). Furthermore, of these 9 large correlation coefficients, 8 are positive and thus confirm our expectations as to the direction in which the explanatory variables push wages. In non-statistical language, wages have (in the main) gone up most rapidly in industries characterized by relatively large increases in employment, relatively large profits, relatively high degrees of industrial concentration, and relatively high degrees of unionization.[1]

Of the four explanatory variables, the level of profits is by far the most consistent in its relationship to wage adjustments. The fact that the correlation coefficient between wage changes and the average level of profits is positive in all six sub-periods means that in *every* sub-period of the 1947-59 period wages went up faster in those industries enjoying relatively high prof-

[1] Perhaps the best way to gauge the overall explanatory power of all four wage-determining variables taken together is by the use of multiple correlation analysis. The multiple correlation coefficients for the six sub-periods under study here are .84, .55, .82, .72, .94, and .73, respectively. With the exception of the coefficient of .55 in the 1949 recession, all of these multiple correlation coefficients are significant at the 5% level, and in the three low unemployment sub-periods the coefficients are significant at the 1% level. These statistics suggest that, in general, the four variables used in this study do explain a reasonably large proportion of inter-industry differences in wage behavior. It is also interesting to note that these four wage-determining variables are relatively more successful in explaining wage behavior in the low unemployment periods than in the recessions.

Inter-Industry Wage Behavior

its than in those industries enjoying relatively low profits.[1]
None of the other wage-determining variables is positively
correlated with changes in wages in every sub-period. However, wages and union strength are positively correlated in five
of the six sub-periods; wages and employment are positively
correlated in four of the six sub-periods (including all three of
the low unemployment periods); and wages and concentration
are positively correlated in three of the six sub-periods (with
the absolute size of the positive correlation coefficients much
larger than the size of the negative correlations).

Furthermore, it is worth noting that while the profit-wage
relationship is the most consistent, it is by no means always the
strongest. In fact, in every sub-period the correlation between
wage adjustments and either employment, concentration, or
union strength is stronger than the correlation between profits
and wages. Hence, in each specific period wage behavior is
dominated to a greater extent by one of the other explanatory
variables than by the profit variable. Apparently all four wage-
determining factors under investigation here have played an
important role in at least some sub-periods.

Let us now see how these initial impressions, based on the
use of simple correlation coefficients, are modified when partial
correlation coefficients are used. Simple correlation coefficients
can, of course, be highly misleading when the explanatory
variables are themselves highly correlated. And this is certainly
the case here, since the highly unionized industries are often
highly concentrated as well, and since these unionized-concen-
trated industries also tend to be the high-profit industries. Consequently, the simple correlation coefficients presented in Table
11 do not really give us an accurate idea of how much each
wage-determining variable *by itself* influences wages. The only
practicable way of testing the effect of each explanatory vari-

---

[1] And, it is very unlikely that this is a "chance" relationship—in three
of the six sub-periods the correlations are significant at the 5% level, and
in two sub-periods the correlations are significant at the 1% level.

TABLE 11

SIMPLE CORRELATION COEFFICIENTS BETWEEN INTER-INDUSTRY WAGE BEHAVIOR AND SELECTED VARIABLES, WITHIN SUB-PERIODS OF 1947-59*

	Simple Correlations Between Wage Changes and—			
Sub-Periods	Percentage Changes in Employment	Average Profit Levels	Concentration Ratios	Unionization Ratios
I.1: Jan. 47-Jan. 49	.48	.21	−.06	.02
(R) I.2: Jan. 49-Oct. 50	.19	.36	−.14	−.36
I.3: Oct. 50-Dec. 53	.44	.64	.54	.74
(R) I.4: Dec. 53-June 55	−.04	.49	.69	.41
I.5: June 55-Aug. 57	.22	.18	−.17	.41
(R) I.6: Aug. 57-June 59	−.49	.60	.72	.22

Notes:
*The 10 percent level of significance is .39; the 5 percent level of significance is .46; and the 1 percent level of significance is .58.
(R) indicates the three recession sub-periods.
Source: See Appendix E.

Inter-Industry Wage Behavior

able on wages when all three of the other variables are held constant is by computing partial correlation coefficients. Table 12 presents the results of some of these computations.[1]

As we might expect, the use of partial correlation coefficients tends (in general) to reduce the size of the correlations. Whereas there were 9 simple correlations between wages and one of the explanatory variables that were large enough to be statistically significant (at the 5% level of significance), there are only 8 partial correlation coefficients that are sufficiently large to merit this distinction. Apparently the use of simple correlations does, in this context, exaggerate the strength of the relationship between wages and each of the four explanatory variables.

The partial correlation analysis also alters our initial impression of the relative importance of the individual wage-determining variables. Most striking is the effect of the partial correlation analysis on the relationship between profits and wages. While wages are still more consistently related to profits than to any of the other wage-determining variables, the strength of the profit-wage relationship—particularly in recent years—is drastically reduced. As the more detailed discussion of the role of the profit variable presented below explains, the apparent relationship between profits and wages in recent years suggested by the simple correlations is attributable to a strong relationship between profits and other wage-determining variables (most notably, concentration).

Many of the other partial correlation coefficients are also lower than the corresponding simple correlation coefficients. In particular, the positive relationship between the degree of unionization and wages has been lowered to such an extent

[1] All of the correlation coefficients (simple, partial, and multiple) relating wage behavior to the four explanatory variables are presented in Appendix E. To avoid overwhelming the reader, only the simple and third-order partial correlation coefficients for Set I sub-periods are presented in the text. The results of the correlations in Set II sub-periods will be brought into the discussion at appropriate points.

TABLE 12

PARTIAL CORRELATION COEFFICIENTS BETWEEN INTER-INDUSTRY WAGE BEHAVIOR AND SELECTED VARIABLES, WITHIN SUB-PERIODS OF 1947-59*

| | | Partial Correlations Between Wage Changes and— | | |
Sub-Periods	Percentage Changes in Employment	Average Profit Levels	Concentration Ratios	Unionization Ratios
I.1: Jan. 47-Jan. 49	.82	.68	.68	—.23
(R) I.2: Jan. 49-Oct. 50	.06	.38	—.18	—.40
I.3: Oct. 50-Dec. 53	—.03	.38	.25	.56
(R) I.4: Dec. 53-June 55	—.23	.00	.56	.18
I.5: June 55-Aug. 57	.90	.09	—.84	.62
(R) I.6: Aug. 57-June 59	.08	.01	.41	—.19

Notes:
*These are third-order partial correlation coefficients; that is, each partial correlation coefficient reports the relationship between wages and the particular explanatory variable under study when all three other explanatory variables are held constant.

The 10 percent level of significance is .43; the 5 percent level of significance is .50; and the 1 percent level of significance is .62.

(R) indicates the three recession sub-periods.

Source: See Appendix E.

Inter-Industry Wage Behavior

that in three of the six sub-periods it now appears as if (when we correct for the effects of the other wage-determining factors) wages went up more rapidly in the weakly unionized industries than in the strongly unionized industries. Not all of the relationships were weakened by holding other variables constant, however. In some sub-periods the partial correlation coefficients between wages and one of the explanatory variables are significantly larger than the simple correlations. Most striking in this respect is the marked upward thrust given to the employment-wage relationship in the low unemployment periods of 1947-48 and 1955-57.

The most systematic way of analyzing and interpreting these (and other) results of the correlation analysis is by examining the relationship between wage behavior and each individual explanatory variable in some detail.

Changes in Employment and Wage Behavior

There is a pronounced cyclical difference in the relationship between inter-industry changes in employment and inter-industry changes in wages. During periods of generally low unemployment, wages have shown a tendency to go up most rapidly in industries characterized by relatively favorable employment trends. That is, industries in which employment has either gone up at a more rapid rate or fallen at a slower rate than employment in the "average" industry have tended to raise wages faster than industries in the opposite circumstances. This pattern does not show up, however, in the recession periods.

In all three low unemployment sub-periods, the simple correlations between changes in employment and changes in wages yield positive results. Furthermore, when we start holding the other wage-determining variables constant, the strength of the positive correlation between changes in employment and changes in wages becomes very pronounced indeed in two of the three low unemployment periods. The partial correlations

Inter-Industry Wage Behavior

between employment and wages are .82 in 1947-48 and .90 in 1955-57—both easily significant at the 1% level. What this seems to indicate is that when labor markets are relatively tight, industries which are trying to increase employment at a relatively rapid rate raise wages faster than industries in which employment is increasing less rapidly (and quite possibly declining).

The only trouble with this intuitively plausible general proposition is that it does not hold in the 1950-53 low unemployment period. While the simple correlation between employment changes and wages is both positive and fairly high (.44, significant at the 5% level), when we begin to allow for the effects of profit levels, concentration, and union strength on wages, the correlation between employment changes and wages disappears (actually, the partial correlation coefficient is −.03). One possible explanation is that in 1950-53, changes in employment, levels of profit, concentration, and unionization were also highly correlated that all of the simple correlation coefficients are reduced by the use of partial correlation.

A less statistical explanation for the lack of a *ceteris paribus* relationship between employment and wages in 1950-53 is that, because of the timing of the Korean War, much of this boom occurred at the tail end of the 1949 recession sub-period and so is lost from sight in the 1950-53 sub-period. Correlations between employment and wages in the recovery phase of the 1949 recession offer strong support for this interpretation—the simple correlation coefficient is .35 and the partial correlation coefficient is .87. Apparently the upsurge in actual and anticipated employment accompanying the Korean War influenced inter-industry wage behavior to a greater extent in the 1949 recovery than in the years between 1950 and 1953.

Turning now to happenings in the recessions, we find that there is no significant relationship between changes in industry employment and wages in any of the three recession sub-periods. This conclusion holds when the employment changes are measured from the start to the end of the recession as well as when employment changes are measured from the start of the recession to the month when unemployment reached its peak. There is simply no evidence that over recessions as a whole wages increase less rapidly in those industries characterized by the sharpest reductions in employment.[1]

Average Profit Levels and
Wage Behavior

The rather remarkable consistency in the relationship between profits and wage increases has already been noted above. In all six sub-periods, the simple correlations between profits and wages are positive. Furthermore, computation of partial correlation coefficients indicates that this steady positive relationship is no statistical freak. No matter what other wage-determining variables are held constant (either singly or in combination with each other), profits and wages are almost invariably positively correlated.[2] Consequently, the *a priori* proposition that high-profit firms are more likely to grant large wage increases than low-profit firms is not contradicted by the postwar experience and in fact receives some significant support.

The reason for not adopting the high profit-high wage hypothesis with greater enthusiasm is that closer scrutiny suggests that in recent years the independent influence of profits

[1] The table of simple correlations reveals a very sizeable *negative* correlation between changes in employment and wages in the 1958 recession. This surprising statistic is directly traceable to a strong negative relationship between changes in employment and industrial concentration and a strong positive relationship between concentration and wage changes. When the partial correlation between employment changes and wages is computed with industrial concentration held constant, the negative relationship does not show up ($r_{we.c} = .09$).

[2] In the whole matrix of simple and partial correlation coefficients relating employment and wages, only two negative coefficients appear. Both of these negative coefficients occur when the degree of unionization is involved in the partial correlations for the 1955-57 period, and both negative coefficients are quite small ($-.07$) and ($-.17$).

Inter-Industry Wage Behavior

on wages (when other variables have been held constant) has been almost nil. Table 12 shows that in the three sub-periods covering the years 1954-59 the partial correlation coefficients relating profit levels and wage changes have been .00, .09, and .01. The statistical explanation for this marked drop in the explanatory power of the profit variable is comparatively simple. Starting with the Korean War sub-period (1950-53), profits have been very highly correlated with concentration ratios and with degree of unionization. In short, the high-profit firms also tend to be the more highly concentrated and the more highly unionized firms.[1]

As soon as we use statistical techniques to dissect this structural relationship by holding concentration and union strength constant while the relationship between variations in profit levels and wages is examined, the independent influence of profits on wages disappears. Apparently the rather large positive correlations between profits and wages in the 1954 and 1958 recessions were the result, not of the independent influence of profits on wages, but of the relationship between concentration, unionization and wages, coupled with the strong relationship between profits and both concentration and unionization.[2]

[1] In the four most recent sub-periods, the simple correlation coefficients relating the level of profits to industrial concentration have been: .42, .66, .54, and .82; all but the first of these coefficients is significant at the 1% level. During these same sub-periods, the simple correlation coefficients relating to the level of profits to the degree of unionization have been: .54, .60, .56, and .46; here all but the last coefficient are significant at the 2% level.

[2] The data contained in a recent study by H. M. Levinson ("Postwar Movement of Prices and Wages in Manufacturing Industries," Study Paper No. 21, Joint Economic Committee, U. S. Congress, 86th Cong., 2d Sess., 1960, pp. 2-5) provide additional support for this interpretation of the role of the profit variable. Levinson's study affords useful corroborative data in that it deals with the same industries analyzed in this monograph, but differs in that it is based on year-to-year changes in wages (and other variables) rather than on variations in wage behavior over sub-periods demarcated by unemployment conditions. Levinson finds the same pattern of high, positive simple correlations between profits and wages evident in Table 11. Levinson himself does not correct for

Inter-Industry Wage Behavior

While the simple relationship between profits and wages in *recent* years is rendered suspect by the use of partial correlation, the same is not true of profit-wage relationships for the earlier periods. In 1947-48, in the 1949 recession, and in 1950-53, the partial correlation coefficients between profits and wages are .68, .38, and .38. Apparently in this earlier period profits exerted an independent influence on wages even after the effects of other wage-determining variables were allowed for.

The key to this difference in the profit-wage relationship between the earlier and the more recent sub-periods may be found in the fact that the low-concentration, low-unionization firms were the high-profit firms in 1947-48, and that even in the 1949 recession and the Korean War period the strength of the positive correlation between profits and concentration was not as high as it has become in more recent years. A possible economic interpretation of these relationships is that when the relatively non-concentrated, non-unionized firms enjoyed the highest profit levels, these firms tended to grant the largest wage increases. However, when these firms as a group were forced to be content with lower profit levels (both absolutely and relative to other manufacturing industries), they no longer provided the largest wage increases—the largest wage increases still tended to go with the most profitable industries, but now the most profitable industries were also the concentrated-unionized industries, and the larger wage increases could be explained by reference to market-power considerations.

the interdependence between high profits, high concentration, and high unionization. However, calculations based on Levinson's data (his concentration ratios differ in certain respects from the concentration ratios used in this study) reveal that correcting for the relationship between profits and concentration reduces his correlation coefficients for 1953-54, 1955-56, 1956-57, and 1957-58 well below the 10% level of significance. Although it is not possible to use Levinson's data to correct for the effects of unionization, the unionization data utilized in the present study suggest strongly that correcting for unionization would also reduce his 1954-55 profit-wage correlation quite markedly.

Inter-Industry Wage Behavior

Industrial Concentration and Wage Behavior

The more highly concentrated industries have produced the largest wage increases in both the 1954 and the 1958 recessions. This conclusion is based on the very high simple correlations between concentration and wages in these two recessions (.69 and .72, both easily significant at the 1% level) and on the inability of partial correlation analysis to eliminate a sizeable part of this positive relationship.

The rather surprising aspect of this relationship is the fact that the partial correlations between concentration and wage adjustments remain so high (.56 and .41). Because of the strong interdependence between the degree of industrial concentration and the average level of profits described above, and because of the widely recognized tendency for high industrial concentration and a high degree of unionization to go together,[1] we might expect that holding profits and the degree of unionization constant would make the remaining relationship between concentration and wages as unnoticeable as the relationship between profits and wages when concentration and unionization were held constant. It is true that allowing for the effects of unionization and profit levels does reduce the strength of the relationship between concentration and inter-industry wage behavior—but the relationship is still very much in evidence. Apparently the existence of a relatively high degree of concentration in the product market can lead to above-average wage increases in an industry even if the degree of unionization and the profit level are only "average."

[1] The simple correlation between industrial concentration and unionization is .46 (significant at the 5% level). Because both the concentration ratios and the unionization ratios are available only for one point of time, we are unable to see how this relationship has varied over years 1947-59. However, both concentration and unionization tend to be rather permanent attributes of broad industry groups, and so it is unlikely that there would be much variation in this correlation coefficient over reasonably short periods.

Inter-Industry Wage Behavior

It must be emphasized that this significant positive relationship between concentration and wages has prevailed only in the last two recessions. The recession-aspect of this relationship suggests that concentrated industries may feel more secure about their future in depressed times and thus be less inclined to put up strenuous resistance to upward wage pressures than industries that are subject to more competition in the product market.

The absence of a significant relationship between concentration and industry wage behavior in the 1949 recession could well be due to the same Korean War "boom" aspects of the recovery period that seem to have been responsible for other "unique" happenings in this first postwar recession. As was noted earlier, wages in the recovery phase of the 1949 recession tended to go up most rapidly in those industries that experienced the most rapid increases in employment, apart from degree of concentration or anything else.

The very peculiar, sharply oscillating, relationship between concentration and wage behavior in the three low unemployment sub-periods is much harder to explain than the recession-relationship. Only 1950-53, in which there was the same fairly large and positive simple correlation along with the much smaller partial correlation that has been noted in the case of every wage-determining variable, requires no special explanation. In 1947-48, the simple correlation between concentration and wages was small and negative, whereas the partial correlation was large and positive. The explanation for this sharp turn-around in the relationship between concentration and wages is that changes in employment and profit levels dominated wage behavior in this period, and the rapidly expanding and most profitable industries were definitely not the highly concentrated industries. Consequently, the wage effects of employment and profit levels swamped the wage effects of concentration and made the simple correlation between wages and concentration unnoticeable. But, when the effects of em-

Inter-Industry Wage Behavior

ployment and profit levels are allowed for, the expected positive relationship between concentration and wage changes is brought to the fore.

The high negative value of the partial correlation between concentration and wages in the 1955-57 investment boom is most difficult of all to explain. Why the more highly concentrated industries (once associated differences in employment, unionization, and profitability have been ruled out) should have experienced smaller wage increases than the less concentrated industries is simply not clear to this writer.

Unionization and Wage Behavior

We have left until last the most widely and heatedly discussed relationship of all—the relationship between the degree of unionization and the rate at which wages in various industries have increased. Possibly the most important conclusion to be drawn about this relationship is a negative conclusion: When the effects of other wage-determining variables are allowed for, there is no simple relationship between unionization and wage behavior. As Table 12 demonstrates, a high degree of unionization per se has been associated with relatively large wage increases in three of the six sub-periods studied and with relatively small wage increases in the other three sub-periods. The simple correlation coefficients in Table 11 indicate the more consistently positive correlation between unionization and wage increases that we would expect on *a priori* grounds. However, the appearance of a direct relationship between unionization and wages in some sub-periods must be attributed to the same interdependence between unionization, concentration, and profitability that has been referred to repeatedly.

This should not be taken to mean that unionization is of no consequence whatsoever for inter-industry differences in wage behavior. During the 1950-53 and 1955-57 sub-periods, the partial correlations between unionization and wage changes are both positive and quite large (.56 and .62, respectively). During both of these sub-periods, wages clearly went up most rapidly in the highly unionized industries. The surprising thing about these relatively high correlations is not that unions seem to have succeeded in raising the wages of their members faster than wages in comparatively non-unionized industries were going up, but that the periods in which this conclusion holds are both low unemployment periods.

If we examine the relationship between unionization and wage changes in the three recession sub-periods, we find that the partial correlations are negative in the 1949 and 1958 recessions and very slightly positive in the 1954 recession. There is apparently no significant relationship between the degree of unionization and wage increases during recessions. The moderately strong and positive relationship suggested by the simple correlations for the 1954 and 1958 recessions is all but wiped out when we allow for the interdependency between unionization, profitability, and concentration.

This evidence suggests strongly that the common view of unionization as a more effective instrument for keeping wages up in depression than for raising wages in relatively prosperous periods needs to be reexamined. Within the manufacturing sector, at any rate, unions seem to be less effective in exerting an independent influence on wages in recessions than in periods of low unemployment.[1]

A word of warning: all of the conclusions in this section

---

[1] The 1947-48 period is clearly an exception to this rule since, in spite of comparatively low unemployment, wages went up more rapidly in non-unionized industries than in unionized industries. The explanation here seems to be that the post-World War II demand pressures were still so strong in this period that the nature of organization on the supplier side of the labor market had little impact on wages; in fact, it has been suggested that the rigidities introduced by union contracts may have actually reduced the rate at which union wages went up. For an excellent discussion of wage behavior in the steel industry during this interesting period, see Albert Rees, "Postwar Wage Determination in the Basic Steel Industry," *American Economic Review*, June 1951, pp. 389-404.

Inter-Industry Wage Behavior

pertain to *inter-industry* variations in wage behavior and must be interpreted with caution. While an analysis of the characteristics of industries in which wages went up at the relatively most rapid rate can (and, in fact, must) be used to form general impressions about the effects of such factors as unionization and concentration on wages in general, inter-industry comparisons often fail to provide conclusive evidence concerning the determinants of the overall wage level. For instance, the fact that in recessions unionization by itself does not seem to explain inter-industry differences in wage behavior cannot be interpreted as conclusive proof that unionization has had no effect on the general level of wages in recessions. It is possible that gains won by unions spread to non-unionized industries, thus raising the general wage level without altering the relationship between union and non-union wage increases.

However, it is also possible to be overly-cautious in drawing conclusions from the available evidence. After all, in two of the three postwar recessions the partial correlations between degree of unionization and industry wage increases were not small and positive (as the wage-transmission hypothesis would suggest), they were *negative*. Furthermore, the extent to which we can expect wage increases in one industry to be transmitted to other industries surely depends on conditions in the labor market—and we would not expect a great deal of wage transmission to occur in recessions, when unemployment is high and profits are declining. Consequently, the fact that wages in different industries are no doubt related to some extent does not cast serious doubt on the main conclusions suggested by the inter-industry comparisons of wage behavior.

The Combined Effect of Concentration and Unionization on Wage Behavior

The above analysis of the independent influence of each individual wage-determining variable gives us some idea of

Inter-Industry Wage Behavior

how wage behavior might be altered if *one* of our four wage-determining variables were to change while the other three stayed roughly constant. While an analysis of this type is indispensable if many questions are to be answered, there are also a number of important questions that can *not* be answered by studying the independent influence of individual wage-determining factors.

For instance, a high degree of industrial concentration and a high degree of unionization tend to occur together in many industries just as low concentration and low unionization tend to characterize other industries. In situations of this sort it may be at least as important to assess the *joint* effects of concentration and unionization taken together as it is to evaluate the independent contributions of concentration and unionization to wage behavior. Looking only at the effects of concentration when unionization is held constant and at the effects of unionization when concentration is held constant may fail to provide a clear picture of the significance of these factors in combination.

Furthermore, from a policy standpoint it may be either inadvisable or politically infeasible to try to alter the degree of market power in either the product or labor market alone. To the extent that our choice lies between trying to change (or regulate) the degree of industrial concentration and the degree of unionization simultaneously or else accepting the status quo in both areas of market power, we must again concentrate on the *combined* effects of concentration and unionization.

There are obviously many combinations of the four individual wage-determining factors that could be studied; however, the close interdependence between concentration and unionization, as well as the special interest of policy-makers in these two aspects of the inflation problem, suggests that the present study concentrate on the joint effects of this pair of factors. Rather than relying exclusively on multiple correlation techniques to sort out these joint effects, it seems more desirable

Inter-Industry Wage Behavior

to deal directly with specific industries that fall clearly into either the high-concentration—high-unionization classification or into the low-concentration—low-unionization category. For this purpose, five industries that rank in approximately the top one-third of all 2-digit manufacturing industries with respect to *both* concentration and unionization have been chosen to constitute the "market-power" sector; five other industries that rank in approximately the bottom one-third of all 2-digit manufacturing industries with respect to *both* concentration and unionization have been chosen to comprise the "competitive" sector. This treatment has the great advantage of providing contrasting sectors that are quite homogeneous with respect to concentration and unionization—that is, we do not deal with the nine remaining 2-digit industries that rank relatively high in concentration but relatively low in unionization, or vice versa.[1]

The main results of a comparison between the "market-power" sector and the "competitive" sector with respect to differences in wage behavior, profit levels, and employment trends are presented in Table 13.

Before analyzing the many differences between the high-concentration—high-unionization sector and the low-concentration—low-unionization sector, one important similarity is worth noting: The three postwar recessions had a very noticeable dampening effect on wage increases in *both* sectors. The downward pressure on average hourly earnings exerted by a relatively long period of relatively high unemployment is not

[1] The phrases "market-power" sector and "competitive" sector must obviously be interpreted loosely and in relative terms. The manufacturing sector as a whole is, of course, considerably more concentrated and more unionized than the economy in general, and this must be kept in mind in interpreting the results of this analysis. The five manufacturing industries placed in the "market-power" sector are: Transportation Equipment, Rubber, Primary Metals, Electrical Machinery, and Stone, Clay, Glass. The five "competitive" industries are: Lumber, Apparel, Furniture, Textiles, and Leather. Appendix D contains the precise concentration and unionization ratios used to select these industries.

Inter-Industry Wage Behavior

confined to the "competitive" sector, but affects highly organized and highly concentrated industries as well.[1]

TABLE 13

TABLE 13

A COMPARISON OF FIVE HIGH-CONCENTRATION—HIGH-UNIONIZATION
INDUSTRIES WITH FIVE
LOW-CONCENTRATION—LOW-UNIONIZATION INDUSTRIES

	(R) Jan.47- Jan.49	Jan.49- Oct.50	(R) Oct.50- Dec.53	Dec.53- June55	(R) June55- Aug.57	Aug.57- June59
Average Percentage Change in Wages in the:						
Market-Power Sector*	9.7	3.6	6.5	3.8	5.3	4.5
Competitive Sector*	7.4	4.4	3.9	1.1	4.6	2.2
Average Percentage Change in Employment in the:						
Market-Power Sector	−3.1	5.6	1.9	0.1	−0.7	−1.3
Competitive Sector	−2.0	5.2	−3.7	1.2	−2.0	1.2
Average Level of Profits in the:						
Market-Power Sector	11.7	13.4	12.8	12.2	14.1	10.7
Competitive Sector	17.1	10.4	7.7	4.9	7.8	6.2

Notes:
*The "market-power" sector contains the following five high-concentration—high-unionization industries: Transportation Equipment, Rubber, Primary Metals, Electrical Machinery, and Stone, Clay, Glass. The "competitive" sector contains the following five low-concentration—low-unionization industries: Leather, Textiles, Furniture, Apparel, and Lumber.
(R) indicates the three recession sub-periods.
Source: Compiled from data in Appendix C.

The most obvious and important difference in wage behavior between the two sectors is that wages have gone up more rapidly in the market-power sector than in the competitive sector in every sub-period of the 1947-59 period but one (the

[1] In fact, the only case in which a recession did *not* dampen wage behavior occurred in the competitive sector—wages went up faster in this sector over the 1949 recession as a whole than over the 1950-53 Korean War boom. However, this peculiarity is no doubt due to the presence of the early parts of the Korean boom in the recovery phase of the 1949 recession and should not be allowed to negate the general proposition that wages in both sectors go up less rapidly in recessions than in low unemployment periods.

Inter-Industry Wage Behavior

eternally troublesome 1949 recession). Consequently, when we combine concentration and unionization (and when we deal only with industries that are rather clearly either "market-power" industries or "competitive" industries) we find a more consistent relationship with industry wage behavior than was apparent when concentration and unionization were studied separately.

Excepting 1947-49, it is also true that profit levels have been significantly higher in the market-power sector than in the competitive sector. This may mean that differences in profit levels also constitute a part of the overall nexus that so consistently has produced larger wage increases for the more concentrated and unionized industries than for the less concentrated and less unionized industries. However, the consistency of the wage pattern in spite of the sharp fluctuations in the magnitude of the profit differential between the two sectors—as well as the negative results of our earlier analysis of the independent influence of profits in recent periods—suggests that the importance of profits in this picture ought not to be exaggerated.

Trends in employment, on the other hand, seem to play no favorites; no particular pattern of employment changes can be identified with either the market-power sector or the competitive sector. The frequent appearance of negative employment changes in both sectors indicates that the intermittent declines in production worker employment that have occurred throughout the postwar period have had their effects on both types of industries. Differences in wage behavior between the high-concentration—high unionization industries and the low-concentration—low-unionization industries certainly can *not* be explained in terms of differences in employment opportunities. If anything, employment has declined more often and more sharply in the market-power sector than in the competitive sector.

A somewhat closer examination of the differences in wage behavior between the two sectors reveals another significant

78

Inter-Industry Wage Behavior

finding: On a proportionate basis, the differences in wage behavior between the two sectors have been greater in the last two recessions than in any other sub-periods. Wages in the high-concentration—high-unionization industries went up more than twice as rapidly in the last two recessions than wages in the more competitive industries.[1]

There is one final difference between happenings in the market-power sector and in the competitive sector that is worth examining. This difference has to do with the differential effect of economic adversity on wage behavior in the two sectors and can be seen more readily in Table 14 than in Table 13.

In Table 14 the identical data presented in Table 13 (for the three recession sub-periods only) have been re-arranged to highlight two sharply contrasting patterns. To appreciate the difference between these patterns it is necessary to make a separate comparison of the relationship between wage behavior, profits, and employment in the market-power sector and in the competitive sector.

Taking the high-concentration—high-unionization sector first, we find a striking *inverse* relationship between the magni-

[1] This conclusion is supported by multiple correlation analysis covering 19 2-digit industries. In the 1954 and 1958 recessions, the multiple correlations between wage changes on the one hand and concentration and unionization on the other hand were .70 and .73, respectively (both values are significant at the 1% level). It is interesting to recall that the third-order partial correlations between unionization and wages (with the other three wage-determining variables held constant) produced a small positive correlation in the 1954 recession and a small negative correlation in the 1958 recession. The partial correlation between industrial concentration and wages, on the other hand, was both fairly large and positive in both recessions. This suggests that concentration may be more significant than unionization in keeping wages up in the highly-concentrated—highly-unionized industries during recessions. Unionization, by way of contrast, appears (on the basis of the partial correlation analysis) to be more significant than concentration in raising wages in the concentrated-unionized industries in good times. However, because of the strong interdependence between concentration and unionization as well as the limited amount of usable experience, too much stress should not be put on these attempts to allocate the joint impact of concentration and unionization.

79

Inter-Industry Wage Behavior

tude of wage increases in the three recessions and the corresponding profit levels and employment trends. Whereas wages went up at the most rapid rate in the 1958 recession and at the slowest rate in the 1949 recession, the trend in employment changes and profit levels over the three recessions is precisely the opposite. Over the 1958 recession, profits were lower than in either of the other two recessions and employment declined; in the 1954 recession profits were somewhat higher than in 1958 and employment was stable; and in the 1949 recession profits were highest and employment increased over the course of the recession.

Turning now to the low-concentration—low-unionization sector, we find a radically different pattern. In this sector, the magnitude of wage increases in the three recessions varied *directly* with profits and employment. In the case of the more competitive industries, the same recession that saw wages go up the most (the 1949 recession) also saw the highest profit levels and the most rapid increase in employment; the recession that witnessed the second largest rate of wage increase (the 1958 recession) also was accompanied by the second highest level of profits and the second (or third, as there is a tie) largest increase in employment; and, in the 1954 recession, when wages went up at the slowest rate in the competitive sector, profits were also at their lowest level and employment changed very little over the course of the recession as a whole.

These two remarkably consistent—and at the same time contrasting—patterns can perhaps be interpreted as follows. Recession wage behavior in the market-power sector does *not* depend to any significant extent on how hard recessions hit either profits or employment in this sector. The 1958 recession inflicted more economic adversity on this particular sector than did any other recession (in the sense that profit levels were lowest and employment declined most rapidly)—and yet wages went up more rapidly in this recession than in either of the two previous recessions. On the other hand, recession wage

Inter-Industry Wage Behavior

TABLE 14

A Comparison of the Relationship Between Wages, Employment, and Profits in the High-Concentration—High-Unionization Sector and in the Low-Concentration—Low-Unionization Sector

Recession Sub-Periods*	High-Concentration—High-Unionization Sector ("Market-Power" Sector)		
	Average Percentage Change in Wages	Average Percentage Change in Employment	Average Level of Profits
Aug. 57-June 59 (1958 Recession)	4.5	−1.3	10.7
Dec. 53-June 55 (1954 Recession)	3.8	0.1	12.2
Jan. 49-Oct. 50 (1949 Recession)	3.6	5.6	13.4

Recession Sub-Periods*	Low-Concentration—Low-Unionization Sector ("Competitive" Sector)		
	Average Percentage Change in Wages	Average Percentage Change in Employment	Average Level of Profits
Jan. 49-Oct. 50 (1949 Recession)	4.4	5.2	10.4
Aug. 57-June 59 (1958 Recession)	2.2	1.2	6.2
Dec. 53-June 55 (1954 Recession)	1.1	1.2	4.9

Notes:
* Listed in order of the size of the average wage change, with the recession associated with the largest percentage change in wages listed first.
Source: Compiled from Table 13.

behavior in the competitive sector seems to be directly and significantly affected by the severity of the impact of the recession on the industries that comprise this sector. The 1954 recession had the harshest impact on profits and employment in the low-concentration—low-unionization industries—and wages responded by going up less rapidly in this recession than in either of the other two recessions.

81

Inter-Industry Wage Behavior

A Brief Re-Interpretation of Wage Behavior in the 1954 and 1958 Recessions

At the start of this chapter the hope was expressed that this analysis of inter-industry wage behavior would throw additional light on one aspect of postwar wage behavior described in Chapter IV, but not altogether explained—namely, the fact that wages in general rose faster during the 1958 recession than during the relatively milder 1954 recession. In Chapter IV two possible explanations were put forth: the behavior of the cost-of-living in the 1958 recession and the timing of key long-term collective bargaining agreements.

The comparison between the market-power and competitive sectors just presented in the preceding section now suggests an additional hypothesis, based on the *incidence* of these two recessions. The essence of this "incidence-of-recessions" hypothesis is that wages in general are likely to rise faster when the brunt of a recession falls on high-concentration—high-unionization industries than when a recession inflicts the greatest economic adversity on the low-concentration—low-unionization sector.

This hypothesis is based on the *a priori* proposition that a decline in business may not have much effect on the wage policies of firms and unions that operate in industries enjoying both relatively high profits and a not-too-competitive product market. A severe cut in profits coupled with a downward trend in the number of production workers needed will, however, cause a firm already experiencing relatively low profits and selling in a competitive product market to exert every effort to prevent average hourly earnings from rising. And, if a sizeable number of the competitive firms also operate in weakly-unionized labor markets, it is likely that this pressure to prevent labor costs from rising will succeed, at least to some extent.

The degree of unionization and concentration in an industry

Inter-Industry Wage Behavior

can also be expected to affect the pattern of recession wage behavior via an institutional channel—namely, the use of long-term collective bargaining agreements. The significance of the long-term contract as an economy-wide phenomenon has already been discussed in Chapter IV; here it is important to add that, for straightforward reasons, long-term contracts containing provisions for "automatic" wage adjustments tend to be much more common within the high-unionization—high-concentration sector of the economy than within the competitive sector. And, it is obvious that industries characterized by the prevalence of long-term contracts have less opportunity to adjust wages to short-term changes in labor market conditions than industries which lack such contractual rigidities.

Whereas the general empirical support for this *a priori* argument is outlined in the above section and need not be recapitulated in detail here, it may be of some interest to see how this incidence-of-recessions hypothesis can be used to provide at least a partial explanation for happenings in the 1954 and 1958 recessions. As was noted above, the 1954 recession had a very sharp impact on the profitability of the low-concentration—low-unionization firms, and the result was a very small increase in average hourly earnings in this sector (1.1%/year); these very moderate wage increases in the competitive sector in turn helped hold down the rate at which the general wage level rose during the 1954 recession.

The 1958 recession, on the other hand, followed on the heels of the 1955-57 boom in the sales of autos, capital goods, and other items produced in the market-power sector, and thus had a relatively strong negative impact on profits and employment in the market-power sector and a relatively mild impact on the competitive sector. The sharp drop in profits in the high-concentration—high-unionization industries had little effect on wages in this sector (in fact, wages in these market-power industries went up slightly faster in the 1958 recession than in 1954); and the relatively mild effect of the 1958 recession on

Inter-Industry Wage Behavior

the competitive sector allowed wages to rise more rapidly in this sector in the 1958 recession than in the 1954 recession. The result: Wages in general went up more rapidly in the 1958 recession than in the 1954 recession.

While it would be imprudent to make too much of this simple incidence-of-recessions hypothesis (many other factors are obviously at work), it does seem that the way in which the brunt of a recession is distributed between industries characterized by high-concentration—high-unionization and industries characterized by low-concentration—low-unionization influences the general behavior of wages in time of recession.

VI. CONCLUSIONS AND POLICY IMPLICATIONS

THIS final chapter will attempt to draw together and interpret the main results of this study of postwar wage behavior. In the first part of the chapter, a brief summary of the principal empirical findings is presented. The second part of the chapter deals with the implications of these findings for monetary-fiscal policy and for other types of anti-inflation policies.

Brief Summary of Principal Findings

It is convenient to summarize the principal empirical findings of this study under four headings: (1) the general relationship between unemployment and wage behavior; (2) variations in the unemployment-wage relationship over time; (3) some general explanations for variations in the unemployment-wage relationship; and (4) inter-industry differences in wage behavior. The reasons for organizing this study around these topics have been explained in the first chapter and need not be repeated here.

The General Relationship Between
Unemployment and Wage Behavior

1. There is a general relationship between the level of unemployment and the rate at which money wages increase: wages rise faster when unemployment is relatively low than when unemployment is relatively high. This conclusion holds for both the long sweep of American economic history (1900-58) and for the post-World War II period considered by itself.

2. There is also, however, a considerable amount of "play" or "looseness" in the general relationship between levels of unemployment and wage increases. This relationship is by no means sufficiently steady and consistent to permit even reasonably accurate predictions of the size of wage increases that will be associated with varying rates of unemployment.

85

Conclusions and Policy Implications

3. In particular, the general relationship between levels of unemployment and wage increases holds only for relatively pronounced and permanent differences in the level of unemployment. While all three postwar recessions have had a definite dampening effect on the size of wage adjustments, there is no evidence that short-run (monthly, bi-monthly, or quarterly) variations in the level of unemployment produce any significant alteration in the behavior of money wages.

4. There is no evidence of any systematic time lag between variations in the level of unemployment and changes in money wages; the "looseness" of the general relationship between unemployment and wage increases cannot be attributed to time lags.

5. A part of this "looseness" is due, however, to the fact that wage behavior is influenced not only by the level of unemployment but also by the *direction* in which unemployment rates are moving. At a given average level of unemployment, wages rise much less rapidly when unemployment is increasing than when unemployment is decreasing. In the postwar period the upward march of wages has been restrained most noticeably in the contraction phases of the three postwar recessions, when unemployment was above 4.3% *and increasing steadily.*

6. The fact that wages are responsive to significant variations in the level of unemployment and to steady increases in the level of unemployment does not mean, however, that wages fall readily. In the three postwar recessions the median rate of increase for average hourly earnings in the manufacturing sector was 3.9%/year; and the median increase in the average wage and salary compensation of all civilian employees was even higher! Only in the contraction phases of the recessions did wages in general fail to go up faster than 2.5%/year.

Variations in the Relationship Between
Unemployment and Wages Over Time

1. A rough comparison of the postwar period with the earlier part of the twentieth century suggests that, at given

Conclusions and Policy Implications

levels of unemployment, wages in the 1947-59 period have gone up somewhat more rapidly than wages in pre-World War II years.

2. The extent of this upward shift in the unemployment-wage relationship must not, however, be exaggerated. In particular, it is important to recognize that the reluctance of wages to fall in spite of considerable unemployment is not solely a recent phenomenon, but has been a characteristic of wage behavior in the United States throughout the twentieth century.

3. *Within* the postwar period, there is less evidence of any broad trend in the overall relationship between unemployment and money wages. On the basis of our limited experience between 1947 and 1959, there is no indication of any upward trend in the rate at which wages increase in times of low unemployment—in fact, wages in the 1955-57 "boom" went up *less* rapidly than wages in either of the two earlier low unemployment periods (1950-53 and 1947-48). Unfortunately, the special characteristics of each of these three low unemployment periods prevents us from predicting with any degree of confidence whether future low unemployment periods will produce smaller or larger wage increases than occurred between 1955 and 1957.

4. In the case of the three postwar recessions, it is clear that wages went up faster in the most recent (1958) recession than in the 1954 recession. However, wages also went up faster in the 1949 recession than in the 1954 recession, thus upsetting any notion of an irreversible upward trend in wage behavior over successive recessions.

5. If we compare only the contraction phases of the three recessions, the hypothesis that wages are increasing ever more rapidly in successive periods receives somewhat more support. Wages increased significantly faster in the contraction phase of the 1958 recession than in the contraction phase of either the 1954 or 1949 recessions. It was the sharp recovery of wages in the recovery phase of the 1949 recession (attributable at

Conclusions and Policy Implications

least in part to the start of the Korean War) that prevents the 1958 recession from standing out as "the" high-wage recession in the postwar period.

General Explanations for Postwar Variations in the Unemployment-Wage Relationship

1. The postwar experience suggests that variations in wage behavior when unemployment is both relatively low and relatively stable depend mainly on the general strength of the aggregate demand for goods and services and on the (related) behavior of the cost-of-living. Wages went up faster in 1947-48 and in 1950-53 than in 1955-57 largely because of the pronounced effects of World War II and the Korean War on general business conditions in the two earlier periods.

2. The explanation for variations in wage behavior between recession periods is not nearly so simple. The rapid rise of wages in the recovery phase of the 1949 recession (mainly as a consequence of the outbreak of hostilities in Korea) demonstrates that a sudden change in general business (and consumer) psychology can have sudden and pronounced effects. The relatively rapid rise of wages in the 1958 recession compared to the 1954 recession suggests a number of more general possibilities.

3. First, a negative conclusion: Broad differences in general profit levels and employment trends do not explain variations in recession wage behavior. Profits were lower and employment (in general) declined more rapidly in the 1958 recession than in the 1954 recession.

4. Happenings in the 1958 recession suggest that the *timing* of key long-term contracts vis-à-vis prosperity periods and the onset of recessions can be quite significant. In addition, the general popularity of long-term contracts can be expected to lessen the dampening influence of recessions on wage adjustments.

Conclusions and Policy Implications

5. The extent to which the cost-of-living goes up also has a bearing on the size of wage increases in recession periods. However, the complex interrelations between wages and prices make it difficult to estimate the independent effect of price behavior on wages. The fact that the Consumer Price Index rose more in the 1958 recession than in the 1954 recession no doubt contributed somewhat to the more rapid rate of wage increase in the 1958 period—but we don't know how much.

6. The results of an inter-industry analysis of wage behavior (summarized in the next section) suggest an incidence-of-recessions hypothesis that is also compatible with the variations in wage behavior between the 1954 and 1958 recessions: Wages in general tend to go up more rapidly when the brunt of a recession is concentrated on the relatively highly-concentrated and highly-unionized industries (the 1958 situation) than when a recession has its greatest impact on industries characterized by relatively strong competition in the product market and a relatively low degree of unionization (the 1954 situation).

Inter-Industry Differences
in Wage Behavior

1. The magnitude of differences in wage behavior between industries must not be exaggerated. The general relationships between unemployment conditions and wage behavior described above hold remarkably well for all types of manufacturing industries. In no industries were average hourly earnings immune from the effects of recessions and steady increases in the level of general unemployment.

2. Within this broad framework of roughly parallel wage changes, some marked differences in industry wage behavior do appear. However, the inter-industry wage pattern is quite complex and most simple, monolithic explanations miss the mark.

Conclusions and Policy Implications

3. Of the four explanatory variables correlated with wage changes in the separate manufacturing industries (rate of change of production-worker employment, average level of profits, degree of concentration, and degree of unionization), profits displayed by far the most consistent relationship to wage adjustments. Profitability was the only variable that was positively correlated with industry wage changes in every one of the six sub-periods studied. Apparently there is a tendency for industries earning relatively high profits to raise wages at a relatively rapid rate, regardless of unemployment conditions.

4. The apparent influence of profits on wages is reduced to a considerable extent, however, when allowance is made for the associated effects of the other wage-determining variables (e.g., concentration and unionization) that are themselves closely correlated with profits. In fact, the *independent* influence of profits on industry wage behavior has been almost nil in the 1954 recession, the 1955-57 boom, and the 1958 recession.

5. The distribution of changes in production-worker employment among manufacturing industries has a pronounced independent effect on inter-industry wage behavior when unemployment is generally low; however, the effect of the general distribution of employment in recessions is not very noticeable.

6. The degree of unionization has much less independent effect on industry wage behavior than the simple correlations between unionization and wages suggest. This is because high degrees of unionization occur most frequently in concentrated, high-profit industries—and both the degree of concentration and the level of profits also affect wages. When both concentration and the level of profits are held constant, the relatively highly unionized firms experienced more rapid increases in average hourly earnings than the relatively weakly unionized manufacturing industries in exactly one-half of the six postwar sub-periods studied.

Conclusions and Policy Implications

7. Still more surprising is the conclusion that unionization has more of a positive effect on industry wages in low unemployment periods than in recessions. When other factors (most notably, concentration) are held constant, there is almost no systematic difference between the behavior of wages in the more strongly unionized industries and in the more weakly unionized industries during the three postwar recessions. In the Korean War period (1950-53) and during the 1955-57 investment boom, on the other hand, unionization per se did have a significant effect on industry wage behavior.

8. In the last two recessions, industry wage behavior has been more closely related to the degree of industrial concentration in various industries than to any other single factor— including unionization. In the main, it has been the relatively concentrated industries that have experienced the largest increases in average hourly earnings during the 1954 and 1958 recessions. On the other hand, concentration does not seem to be positively related to industry wage behavior in low unemployment periods.

9. In industries which are *both* highly concentrated and highly unionized, average hourly earnings have a strong tendency to rise more rapidly than earnings in the low-concentration—low-unionization sector, regardless of the unemployment conditions. The joint effects of concentration and unionization may be greater than the algebraic sum of their individual effects. Another significant difference between these two broad sectors is that recession wage behavior in the relatively concentrated and unionized sector is much less influenced by the direct incidence of recessions on member firms than is wage behavior in the competitive sector; and this pattern suggests the broad hypothesis about general wage behavior in recessions that was mentioned earlier.

91

Conclusions and Policy Implications

Policy Implications

No analysis of wage behavior can hope to provide a definitive statement of the "right" mix of anti-inflation policies. Such a definitive statement would require not only a more comprehensive study of wage behavior than has been attempted here, but also: an analysis of the relationship between wages, productivity, and costs; a thorough investigation of industry price behavior; an appreciation of the effects of the various instruments of monetary-fiscal policy on aggregate demand; an understanding of the likely consequences of alternative policies designed to modify the workings of our economic institutions; and, finally, detailed knowledge of the goals of our society and how much of one goal we are prepared to sacrifice in order to move an extra step toward the attainment of other policy objectives.

All that the present study can contribute to this awesome tableau of needed information is some notion of the likely effects of monetary-fiscal policies on wages and some idea of whether any simple policy alternatives promise better results.

Implications for Monetary-Fiscal Policies

Some of the recent talk about "cost inflation" as a unique problem falling beyond the pale of traditional monetary-fiscal policies notwithstanding, monetary-fiscal policies, by influencing the general level of economic activity, can—and inevitably do—affect wage behavior. The rate at which wages increase does depend on conditions in the labor market (approximated by the rate of unemployment), and general monetary-fiscal policies most certainly can be used to affect conditions in the labor market.

Controlling wage behavior by means of monetary-fiscal policies is not a painless process, however. Decreases in the rate at which wages increase are likely to be achieved only at the cost of some additional amount of unemployment. The empirical findings of this study definitely suggest the existence of a policy

Conclusions and Policy Implications

dilemma in that wages in general continue to go up faster than a rough index of output per man-hour even when unemployment is above the non-frictional level. Hence the monetary-fiscal authorities do indeed face a situation in which labor costs are likely to rise before full employment is reached. No amount of "faith" in the American economy can alter this harsh fact.

Unfortunately, the wage behavior aspect of this dilemma is complicated by the absence of a nice, neat, and continuous functional relationship between the level of unemployment and the magnitude of wage adjustments. We simply cannot tell with precision how much effect a given variation in the level of unemployment will have on wages. However, investigation of the unemployment-wage relationship does suggest that:

1) It will take a very considerable amount of unemployment to prevent wages from rising faster than output per man-hour—historically, the "normal" rate of wage increase has been larger than 2.5%/annum whenever unemployment has been below 9% of the nonfarm labor force.

2) Short-run variations in the level of unemployment are likely to have very little effect on wages—it takes a relatively permanent spell of high unemployment (i.e., a recession) to have a pronounced dampening effect on the rate at which wages increase.

3) What really reduces the rate at which wages advance is a period when unemployment is both relatively high and increasing steadily—the contraction phase of the business cycle is the time when increases in average hourly earnings are significantly arrested.

4) Since so much of the effect of unemployment conditions on wages comes from steady *increases* in the level of unemployment, it is by no means clear

93

Conclusions and Policy Implications

how much of a difference in wage behavior is associated with relatively small variations in the *level* of unemployment.

All of the above comments pertain, of course, to the relationship between unemployment and wages that has prevailed in the recent past, and this relationship may change as policies and institutions change. While there is evidence that, at given levels of unemployment, wages in the postwar period have risen more rapidly than wages in earlier years, there is no evidence of any strong, irresistible upward trend in the unemployment-wage relationship within the postwar period. Consequently, the shift in the pattern of wage behavior between the prewar and postwar periods may have been largely a once-and-for-all shift and need not necessarily herald future upward shifts in this relationship. On the other hand, there are certainly no known reasons for expecting that in the future wages will go up less rapidly (at given levels of unemployment) than they have in the past.

Some have suggested that if the monetary-fiscal authorities made it quite plain that they intended to prevent inflation no matter what the cost in terms of unemployment and growth, this firm stand would by itself remove the apparent policy dilemma. This position is based on the hope that wage- and price-setters can be taught that an attempt to impose inflation on the economy will result in lower real incomes all around—*and* that this lesson will persuade them to cease anti-social behavior and conform to the stable-price mores of the country.

Such a rigid and all-embracing commitment to the goal of price stability has never been attempted, and so it is impossible to either support or rebut this line of reasoning by marshalling conclusive empirical proof. However, there are substantial *a priori* reasons for doubting that, in any economy where wage and price decisions are decentralized, a tough monetary-fiscal policy will make it unprofitable for *individual* firms and unions

94

Conclusions and Policy Implications

to raise their own rates of compensation faster than the requirements of price stability allow.

Consequently, we are forced to conclude that—given the present institutional fabric of our society—the dilemma between low unemployment and labor-cost stability is real indeed and does not seem likely to disappear of its own volition in the near future. The significance of current patterns of wage behavior for monetary-fiscal policy is that the tendency of labor costs to rise in spite of non-frictional unemployment contributes to the hard choice between anti-inflation and anti-unemployment policies.

Implications for Other Types
of Anti-Inflation Policy

Being forced to choose between two desirable objectives of public policy is obviously undesirable, and so the question naturally arises: Is there any way in which the dilemma facing the monetary-fiscal authorities can be removed (or at least lessened) by altering other aspects of the economy? The only direct answer that can be given to this question, on the basis of present information, is that there are no simple panaceas or obvious institutional reforms that will make price stability and full employment perfectly compatible.

The rather remarkable uniformity in the way wages in all kinds of industries have been affected by general unemployment conditions suggests the absence of glaring differences in wage behavior as a consequence of unionization, concentration, and the like. The detailed analysis of inter-industry variations in wage behavior (at given levels of unemployment), while revealing some highly interesting and significant differences in patterns of wage behavior among industries, also failed to unearth any reasonably strong and consistent relationship between wage behavior and any single wage-determining factor.

There is no question but that "imperfections" in product and labor markets accentuate the rate at which wages increase.

Conclusions and Policy Implications

However, the empirical results of this study suggest that the significance of both unionization and industrial concentration has probably been exaggerated in many discussions of the inflation problem. For one thing, the historical evidence shows that wages were by no means perfectly "flexible" in the days before strong trade unionism made important inroads in the industrial sector. And, the more detailed investigation of postwar wage behavior also warns against attributing too large a part of recession wage increases to unionization. Industrial concentration seems to be somewhat more important than unionization in influencing recession wage behavior, but in "good times" the influence of this factor on wages diminishes.

Consequently, it does not seem that even the wholesale elimination of trade unionism and industrial concentration—on the Herculean assumption that such a thing were possible—would solve the wage behavior aspect of the inflation-unemployment dilemma. Furthermore, it is important to recognize that both unionization and some degree of industrial concentration may perform other worthwhile functions in society. Even if unions could be convicted of primary responsibility for our inflation problem, we might want to maintain reasonably strong trade unionism as a method of protecting the individual worker from arbitrary and capricious actions in the course of his regular employment. Similarly, there are reasons for thinking that reasonably large aggregates of industrial power are helpful in stimulating growth and innovation.

The above cautious comments are certainly not intended as any "whitewash" of industrial concentration and unionization. It is quite clear that wages in the high-concentration—high-unionization sector have shown more of a tendency to go up under all unemployment conditions than wages in the more "competitive" areas of manufacturing. Consequently, it is entirely proper that we continue to seek methods of preventing wage and price behavior in the "market-power" industries from getting out of line and raising the overall price level. Various

Conclusions and Policy Implications

specific possibilities, such as public review boards and congressional scrutiny, have been suggested and merit careful consideration.

Other, more general, suggestions (including proposals for allowing fuller reign to foreign competition and for increasing the mobility of workers out of relatively depressed areas and occupations) may also help in the battle against inflation. A final possibility is, of course, the institution of comprehensive wage and price controls; however, the economic and political disadvantages of this type of remedy seem to far outweigh the seriousness of the problem itself.

This writer is thus led to the conclusion that, while various special policy measures may help somewhat to reduce the scope of the problem, main responsibility for the prevention of both large-scale unemployment and serious inflation must continue to rest on the traditional tools of monetary-fiscal policy. The likelihood that these traditional tools will not succeed fully in achieving both low unemployment and complete price stability should be frankly recognized. However, the probable margin of failure does not seem so great as to suggest the need for a radical overhauling of our entire institutional framework. At this juncture, it is probably wisest to adjust monetary and fiscal policies to the realities of the day as best we can. What is needed is neither pious expressions of faith in the ability of the economy to solve all problems nor counsels of total despair, but rather a tough-minded and continuing effort to find the best possible balance between our conflicting objectives.

APPENDIX A

Annual Wage and Unemployment Data, 1900-1958

Sources:

The unemployment data for 1900-1954 are from Stanley Lebergott, "Annual Estimates of Unemployment in the United States, 1900-1954," National Bureau of Economic Research, *The Measurement and Behavior of Unemployment* (Princeton, N.J.: Princeton University Press, 1957), pp. 215-216. Comparable nonfarm unemployment rates for 1955-1958 were kindly supplied by Mr. Lebergott. Civilian labor force unemployment data for 1955-1958 are from U.S. Department of Commerce, *Business Statistics*, 1959, p. 59.

The wage data measure annual percentage changes in the average hourly earnings of production workers in manufacturing, and are from Clarence D. Long, "The Illusion of Wage Rigidity: Long and Short Cycles in Wages and Labor Costs," *Review of Economics and Statistics*, May 1960, pp. 160-161.

Methodological Note:

The wage change indicated for year t is defined as $\dfrac{W_{t+1} - W_t}{W_t}$. Since the wage figure for a given year must be taken to represent the wage at the mid-point of that year, this convention means that the wage change indicated for 1916, for example, really represents the wage change that occurred between mid-1916 and mid-1917. This amounts to introducing a six-month lag into the relationship between unemployment and wage changes.

Appendix A

	Annual percentage change in wages	Unemployment as a percent of nonfarm employees	Unemployment as a percent of the total civilian labor force
1900	4.4	8.7	5.0
1901	4.2	4.3	2.4
1902	3.5	4.5	2.7
1903	—4.5	4.4	2.6
1904	4.0	7.9	4.8
1905	7.8	5.1	3.1
1906	3.6	1.4	0.8
1907	—4.0	2.9	1.8
1908	0.5	13.5	8.5
1909	5.7	8.2	5.2
1910	2.0	9.1	5.9
1911	1.4	9.5	6.2
1912	5.7	7.9	5.2
1913	0.0	6.4	4.4
1914	3.1	11.9	8.0
1915	16.1	14.3	9.7
1916	17.6	7.1	4.8
1917	26.4	7.0	4.8
1918	20.2	2.1	1.4
1919	22.0	3.4	2.3
1920	—9.5	5.8	4.0
1921	—6.8	16.9	11.9
1922	6.3	10.9	7.6
1923	4.8	4.6	3.2
1924	0.0	8.0	5.5
1925	0.2	5.9	4.0
1926	0.4	2.8	1.9
1927	2.2	5.9	4.1
1928	0.7	6.4	4.4
1929	—2.5	4.7	3.2
1930	—6.7	13.0	8.9
1931	—13.4	23.3	15.9
1932	—0.9	34.0	23.6
1933	20.4	35.3	24.9
1934	3.4	30.6	21.7
1935	1.1	28.4	20.1
1936	12.2	23.9	17.0
1937	0.5	20.0	14.3
1938	1.0	26.4	19.0
1939	4.4	23.8	17.2
1940	10.3	20.2	14.6
1941	17.0	13.3	9.9
1942	12.7	6.3	4.7
1943	6.0	2.5	1.9
1944	0.4	1.6	1.2
1945	6.2	2.5	1.9
1946	13.9	5.2	3.9

100

Appendix A

	Annual percentage change in wages	Unemployment as a percent of nonfarm employees	Unemployment as a percent of the total civilian labor force
1947	9.2	4.7	3.6
1948	3.8	4.5	3.4
1949	4.6	7.3	5.5
1950	8.5	6.6	5.0
1951	5.0	3.8	3.0
1952	6.0	3.4	2.7
1953	2.3	3.2	2.5
1954	3.9	6.3	5.0
1955	5.3	5.0	4.0
1956	4.6	4.7	3.8
1957	2.9	5.3	4.3
1958	4.2	8.4	6.8

APPENDIX B

Average Compensation of the Civilian Labor Force,
Seasonally Adjusted Monthly Totals at Annual Rates

Source:

This aggregative wage series is based on (1) seasonally
adjusted national income data compiled from U.S. Department
of Commerce, *U.S. Income and Output*, 1959, Tables I-9 and
II-3, and from recent issues of the *Survey of Current Business*;
and (2) seasonally adjusted total civilian employee data provided by the Bureau of Labor Statistics.

Monthly totals for total annual compensation of civilian
employees were obtained by, first, assuming that "military"
compensation and "supplements" to wages and salaries are
constant during each month of a given quarter. The monthly
total compensation series was then constructed by taking the
monthly sum of wage and salary disbursements, subtracting
the appropriate quarterly "military" compensation figure, and
adding the appropriate quarterly "supplements" figure. These
figures were then divided by the monthly total civilian employment data to obtain a monthly series showing average compensation of civilian employees at annual rates.

Methodological Note:

Since these data were computed, the Bureau of Labor
Statistics has introduced a new set of seasonally adjusted
employment data, based on revised seasonal adjustment factors.
Consequently, the data presented below cannot be extended
beyond 1958 without sacrificing comparability unless all the
data are recomputed using the new seasonally adjusted employment series (available in *Survey of Current Business*, April
1960, p. 23).

Appendix B

AVERAGE COMPENSATION OF THE CIVILIAN LABOR FORCE,
SEASONALLY ADJUSTED MONTHLY TOTALS AT ANNUAL RATES
1947-1958
(IN DOLLARS)

	Jan.	Feb.	Mar.	Apr.	May	June	July	Aug.	Sept.	Oct.	Nov.	Dec.
1947	2114	2112	2113	2113	2121	2145	2129	2160	2183	2193	2229	2254
1948	2248	2248	2271	2256	2317	2306	2324	2357	2369	2371	2372	2358
1949	2365	2351	2320	2361	2361	2352	2340	2332	2324	2310	2298	2341
1950	2364	2352	2392	2408	2438	2466	2506	2536	2588	2590	2621	2675
1951	2704	2747	2754	2792	2796	2867	2814	2834	2860	2860	2908	2904
1952	2923	2954	2989	2966	2972	2985	2962	3043	3072	3122	3118	3126
1953	3119	3144	3160	3190	3226	3215	3221	3231	3243	3236	3227	3241
1954	3233	3212	3213	3218	3233	3246	3249	3246	3236	3255	3289	3302
1955	3309	3332	3347	3367	3393	3405	3442	3409	3427	3440	3459	3465
1956	3481	3511	3537	3570	3563	3589	3584	3615	3641	3668	3686	3723
1957	3737	3726	3728	3750	3777	3794	3799	3834	3825	3807	3814	3791
1958	3793	3781	3783	3778	3791	3852	3953	3897	3918	3897	3940	3956

APPENDIX C

Wage, Profit, and Employment Data for 2-Digit
Manufacturing Industries, Within Sub-Periods of 1947-59

Tables C-1 through C-21 in this Appendix present wage, profit, and employment data for manufacturing as a whole and for 20 2-digit major industry groups (defined according to the 1947 Standard Industrial Classification) within the manufacturing sector. Table C-22 presents wage and employment data for all civilian employees. The sources and methods used in compiling these tables are described below.

Wage Data

Sources:

The wage data for all manufacturing industries measure average hourly earnings paid production or non-supervisory employees and have been taken from summary sheets kindly supplied by the Bureau of Labor Statistics.[1]

The wage data presented for all civilian employees (Table C-22) measure average compensation (including supplements) of all civilian employees, and are seasonally adjusted. These data have been derived from the data in Appendix *B* by the methods outlined below.

[1] These wage data are not seasonally adjusted, and to the best of this writer's knowledge no seasonally adjusted data for average hourly earnings in 2-digit manufacturing industries are published. However, because these data measure average *hourly* earnings, we would not expect the common seasonal variations in total employment and the length of the work-week to cause any serious difficulties. Casual inspection of the wage series for all manufacturing and for several of the 2-digit industries failed to reveal any noticeable seasonal pattern. An earlier study by the National Bureau of Economic Research (Daniel Creamer, "Behavior of Wage Rates During Business Cycles," Occasional Paper No. 34, 1950, p. 36) also suggests that average hourly earnings data are not subject to any very significant seasonal variations. Consequently, for both *a priori* and empirical reasons, it seems highly unlikely that the results of this study are distorted in any significant sense by the unavailability of seasonally adjusted data.

Appendix C

Methods:

The wage series presented in the following tables were constructed in two steps. First, the simple percentage change in wages during each sub-period was calculated. Second, these simple percentage changes for each sub-period were multiplied by a factor based on the number of months in the sub-period $\left[\dfrac{12}{\text{No. of months in sub-period}} \right]$ in order to convert the simple percentage wage increases in all sub-periods to annual rates. This second step was necessary to permit a comparison of wage behavior between sub-periods of unequal duration.

Employment Data

Sources:

The employment data for the manufacturing industries measure the total number of production or non-supervisory employees and are seasonally adjusted. These data have been taken from summary sheets kindly supplied by the Bureau of Labor Statistics.

The employment data for all civilian employees measure total civilian employment and are seasonally adjusted. These data have also been taken from summary sheets supplied by the Bureau of Labor Statistics.

Methods:

The employment series presented in the following tables have been constructed in exactly the same manner as the wage series described above.

Profits Data

Source:

The profits data for the manufacturing industries measure the average rate of return on stockholders' equity after taxes (at annual rates) and have been taken from various issues of

Appendix C

a joint publication of the Federal Trade Commission and the Securities and Exchange Commission entitled: *Quarterly Financial Report for Manufacturing Corporations.*

Methods:

The raw profits data available are not ideally suited to the needs of this study for two reasons: (1) they measure quarterly levels of profits instead of monthly levels; (2) they are not seasonally adjusted, in spite of the marked seasonal variations in the profit patterns of some industries.[1]

Since the major objective here was a measure of the average profit level in each industry over each sub-period, it was decided to meet both of the above difficulties by approximating each sub-period with some multiple of four consecutive quarters. The four (or eight, or twelve) quarters averaged to obtain the profit figure for each sub-period do not, of course, coincide perfectly with the monthly boundaries of all subperiods. However, in most cases the time periods covered by the profits data and the time periods marked off by unemployment conditions and covered by the wage and employment data coincide remarkably well. In the case of all sub-periods, every effort was made not only to match the time periods as closely as possible, but also to see that where slight discrepancies in coverage were unavoidable the particular quarters averaged to obtain the profits figure were representative of the unemployment conditions in the sub-period.

As a result of (1) the reasonably long duration of most subperiods, (2) the fact that the profit figure being computed was an average of at least four quarterly figures, and (3) some good luck in the timing of the postwar recessions—this make-shift approach does not seem to raise any serious questions about

---

[1] A third difficulty is that there are three discontinuities in the sample of firms represented in the profits data over the period 1947-59. However, these discontinuities result in such very small changes in average profit levels within the broad 2-digit industry groupings that they can be disregarded without serious risk.

Appendix C

the usefulness of the profits data. A full listing of the quarterly sub-periods used for measuring average profits in each regular sub-period is available upon request.

A measure of the algebraic change in average profits over the course of each sub-period was also calculated. To avoid seasonal problems, it was necessary to compare the profit rate in a given quarter of one year with the profit rate in the identical quarter of another year. Again, every effort was made to see that the specific quarters chosen to approximate each sub-period coincided as closely as possible with the monthly boundary dates of the sub-periods. Because only two quarters were involved in these calculations, this series is not as reliable as the series measuring average profit levels throughout each sub-period. The estimates of the algebraic change in average profits were therefore used sparingly in this study.

TABLE C-1

Basic Data: All Manufacturing

Sub-Periods	Percentage change in average hourly earnings*	Percentage change in production worker employment*	Average rate of return on stockholders' equity (after taxes)	Change in rate of return on stockholders' equity* (after taxes)
Set I:				
1. Jan. 47-Jan. 49	9.9	—2.4	12.0	—1.8
2. Jan. 49-Oct. 50	3.9	3.5	13.4	0.5
3. Oct. 50-Dec. 53	6.3	0.5	11.5	—2.2
4. Dec. 53-May 55	2.8	—0.8	9.9	0.8
5. May 55-Sept. 57	4.8	—0.9	12.3	—0.6
6. Sept. 57-Jan. 59	4.4	—0.8	9.6	—0.5
Set II:				
1. Jan. 49-Nov. 49	—1.1	—10.4	11.6	—4.8
2. Nov. 49-Oct. 50	8.5	17.8	14.2	5.2
3. Dec. 53-Sept. 54	0.4	—8.8	9.7	—1.6
4. Sept. 54-May 55	5.0	8.7	10.1	4.5
5. Sept. 57-Aug. 58	2.6	—10.7	8.2	—1.6
6. Aug. 58-June 59	6.2	11.2	10.6	0.7

* At annual rates.

TABLE C-2
ORDNANCE AND ACCESSORIES

Sub-Periods	Percentage change in average hourly earnings*	Percentage change in production worker employment*	Average rate of return on stockholders' equity (after taxes)	Change in rate of return on stockholders' equity (after taxes)*
Set I:				
1. Jan. 47-Jan. 49	6.6	4.5	n.a.	n.a.
2. Jan. 49-Oct. 50	6.8	9.5	n.a.	n.a.
3. Oct. 50-Dec. 53	6.9	159.0	n.a.	n.a.
4. Dec. 53-May 55	3.7	−30.9	n.a.	n.a.
5. May 55-Sept. 57	7.2	−9.0	n.a.	n.a.
6. Sept. 57-June 59	4.6	−1.5	n.a.	n.a.
Set II:				
1. Jan. 49-Nov. 49	5.8	−20.0	n.a.	n.a.
2. Nov. 49-Oct. 50	7.4	43.6	n.a.	n.a.
3. Dec. 53-Sept. 54	3.1	−50.5	n.a.	n.a.
4. Sept. 54-May 55	1.5	−14.2	n.a.	n.a.
5. Sept. 57-Aug. 58	5.0	−11.7	n.a.	n.a.
6. Aug. 58-June 59	3.8	10.8	n.a.	n.a.

* At annual rates.

TABLE C-3
Food and Kindred Products

Sub-Periods	Percentage change in average hourly earnings*	Percentage change in production worker employment*	Average rate of return on stockholders' equity (after taxes)	Change in rate of return on stockholders' equity (after taxes)*
Set I:				
1. Jan. 47-Jan. 49	9.0	−2.2	15.2	−3.0
2. Jan. 49-Oct. 50	3.4	−1.1	12.1	−0.5
3. Oct. 50-Dec. 53	7.2	−0.5	8.3	−1.4
4. Dec. 53-May 55	3.9	−0.8	8.1	0.7
5. May 55-Sept. 57	4.2	−2.1	9.0	−0.3
6. Sept. 57-June 59	5.4	−0.4	8.9	0.0
Set II:				
1. Jan. 49-Nov. 49	1.1	−2.5	11.8	−1.9
2. Nov. 49-Oct. 50	5.6	0.2	12.2	0.9
3. Dec. 53-Sept. 54	0.0	−3.2	7.8	−1.3
4. Sept. 54-May 55	8.2	1.8	8.5	3.1
5. Sept. 57-Aug. 58	3.4	−2.1	8.4	−0.5
6. Aug. 58-June 59	7.3	1.6	9.2	0.7

* At annual rates.

TABLE C-4

TOBACCO

Sub-Periods	Percentage change in average hourly earnings*	Percentage change in production worker employment*	Average rate of return on stockholders' equity (after taxes)	Change in rate of return on stockholders' equity (after taxes)*
Set I:				
1. Jan. 47-Jan. 49	5.3	—6.0	12.0	0.6
2. Jan. 49-Oct. 50	3.7	—5.5	12.0	—2.7
3. Oct. 50-Dec. 53	6.3	0.7	9.1	—0.4
4. Dec. 53-May 55	8.5	—2.3	10.1	0.4
5. May 55-Sept. 57	1.5	—3.3	11.7	0.0
6. Sept. 57-June 59	11.0	—3.4	13.5	0.3
Set II:				
1. Jan. 49-Nov. 49	2.8	—8.2	12.6	—3.8
2. Nov. 49-Oct. 50	4.5	—3.4	11.9	—1.7
3. Dec. 53-Sept. 54	—0.6	—2.8	10.0	1.2
4. Sept. 54-May 55	19.3	—1.6	10.6	2.5
5. Sept. 57-Aug. 58	10.9	—8.9	13.4	0.7
6. Aug. 58-June 59	10.6	3.1	13.8	—0.1

* At annual rates.

TABLE C-5
TEXTILES

Sub-Periods	Percentage change in average hourly earnings*	Percentage change in production worker employment*	Average rate of return on stockholders' equity (after taxes)	Change in rate of return on stockholders' equity (after taxes)*
Set I:				
1. Jan. 47-Jan. 49	11.2	—3.1	19.2	—5.0
2. Jan. 49-Oct. 50	4.7	3.3	10.1	0.2
3. Oct. 50-Dec. 53	1.8	—6.3	6.8	—4.0
4. Dec. 53-May 55	0.5	—2.5	1.9	0.2
5. May 55-Sept. 57	4.0	—2.4	5.6	—0.3
6. Sept. 57-June 59	2.6	—2.2	4.6	1.6
Set II:				
1. Jan. 49-Nov. 49	—0.2	—2.2	7.6	—5.8
2. Nov. 49-Oct. 50	9.2	8.4	11.3	5.7
3. Dec. 53-Sept. 54	—0.5	—3.2	1.8	—4.1
4. Sept. 54-May 55	2.2	—1.6	3.8	5.1
5. Sept. 57-Aug. 58	0.0	—6.4	3.0	0.4
6. Aug. 58-June 59	5.5	2.6	6.2	3.0

* At annual rates.

TABLE C-8
FURNITURE

Sub-Periods	Percentage change in average hourly earnings*	Percentage change in production worker employment*	Average rate of return on stockholders' equity (after taxes)	Change in rate of return on stockholders' equity (after taxes)*
Set I:				
1. Jan. 47-Jan. 49	8.6	—0.8	17.2	—2.8
2. Jan. 49-Oct. 50	4.4	10.3	11.6	4.1
3. Oct. 50-Dec. 53	5.9	—3.5	10.8	—5.1
4. Dec. 53-May 55	1.3	2.8	5.9	3.2
5. May 55-Sept. 57	4.5	1.2	10.7	0.7
6. Sept. 57-June 59	1.9	2.2	7.3	1.1
Set II:				
1. Jan. 49-Nov. 49	0.4	—0.5	8.1	—4.3
2. Nov. 49-Oct. 50	8.0	20.1	12.3	11.8
3. Dec. 53-Sept. 54	0.4	0.0	4.8	—0.9
4. Sept. 54-May 55	1.9	6.0	7.0	7.9
5. Sept. 57-Aug. 58	0.7	—4.5	5.7	—1.1
6. Aug. 58-June 59	3.4	9.8	8.7	3.7

* At annual rates.

TABLE C-9

PAPER

Sub-Periods	Percentage change in average hourly earnings*	Percentage change in production worker employment*	Average rate of return on stockholders' equity (after taxes)	Change in rate of return on stockholders' equity (after taxes)*
Set I:				
1. Jan. 47-Jan. 49	11.4	-0.8	19.2	-2.8
2. Jan. 49-Oct. 50	4.4	4.7	13.4	3.9
3. Oct. 50-Dec. 53	6.2	0.6	12.5	-3.7
4. Dec. 53-May 55	3.7	1.1	9.9	0.7
5. May 55-Sept. 57	6.4	0.4	11.2	-1.2
6. Sept. 57-June 59	3.3	0.0	8.2	0.5
Set II:				
1. Jan. 49-Nov. 49	1.9	-1.2	10.7	-1.0
2. Nov. 49-Oct. 50	6.5	10.1	14.2	8.3
3. Dec. 53-Sept. 54	2.2	-1.2	9.7	-0.9
4. Sept. 54-May 55	3.5	3.7	10.5	3.1
5. Sept. 57-Aug. 58	2.6	-3.2	7.4	-1.4
6. Aug. 58-June 59	4.0	3.6	9.0	2.0

* At annual rates.

TABLE C-10

PRINTING

Sub-Periods	Percentage change in average hourly earnings*	Percentage change in production worker employment*	Average rate of return on stockholders' equity (after taxes)	Change in rate of return on stockholders' equity* (after taxes)
Set I:				
1. Jan. 47-Jan. 49	12.5	—1.5	16.0	—1.6
2. Jan. 49-Oct. 50	5.0	0.7	11.5	—0.2
3. Oct. 50-Dec. 53	5.2	1.6	9.9	—0.9
4. Dec. 53-May 55	3.1	1.5	9.2	1.1
5. May 55-Sept. 57	3.3	2.5	11.9	1.8
6. Sept. 57-June 59	3.8	—0.2	9.7	1.7
Set II:				
1. Jan. 49-Nov. 49	5.9	—1.7	11.4	—4.2
2. Nov. 49-Oct. 50	3.9	3.0	10.8	3.5
3. Dec. 53-Sept. 54	1.4	1.6	8.8	—1.3
4. Sept. 54-May 55	3.9	1.5	9.5	4.1
5. Sept. 57-Aug. 58	3.1	—2.0	9.3	—0.4
6. Aug. 58-June 59	4.4	1.8	10.0	4.0

* At annual rates.

TABLE C-11

CHEMICALS

Sub-Periods	Percentage change in average hourly earnings*	Percentage change in production worker employment*	Average rate of return on stockholders' equity (after taxes)	Change in rate of return on stockholders' equity (after taxes)*
Set I:				
1. Jan. 47-Jan. 49	10.9	—1.4	16.0	—0.2
2. Jan. 49-Oct. 50	5.4	0.0	15.5	0.7
3. Oct. 50-Dec. 53	6.9	1.6	11.4	—2.4
4. Dec. 53-May 55	4.2	1.6	11.6	2.0
5. May 55-Sept. 57	5.8	—1.0	14.3	—0.4
6. Sept. 57-June 59	4.3	—0.4	12.5	0.6
Set II:				
1. Jan. 49-Nov. 49	2.3	—9.1	13.2	—1.4
2. Nov. 49-Oct. 50	8.0	8.9	17.2	2.6
3. Dec. 53-Sept. 54	2.4	—3.5	10.9	0.9
4. Sept. 54-May 55	3.9	7.4	12.9	6.0
5. Sept. 57-Aug. 58	4.4	—5.5	11.4	—1.2
6. Aug. 58-June 59	4.0	6.0	13.3	2.9

* At annual rates.

TABLE C-12

PRODUCTS OF PETROLEUM AND COAL

Sub-Periods	Percentage change in average hourly earnings*	Percentage change in production worker employment*	Average rate of return on stockholders' equity (after taxes)	Change in rate of return on stockholders' equity (after taxes)*
Set I:				
1. Jan. 47-Jan. 49	13.9	—2.5	17.2	—2.4
2. Jan. 49-Oct. 50	2.9	—0.3	12.8	0.0
3. Oct. 50-Dec. 53	6.6	—0.3	11.0	—4.7
4. Dec. 53-May 55	3.1	—3.5	6.2	—0.1
5. May 55-Sept. 57	6.7	—1.7	8.7	—0.8
6. Sept. 57-June 59	3.1	3.1	10.3	—0.7
Set II:				
1. Jan. 49-Nov. 49	1.6	—1.9	11.9	—7.7
2. Nov. 49-Oct. 50	3.9	1.2	12.2	7.0
3. Dec. 53-Sept. 54	2.0	—5.1	6.2	—0.4
4. Sept. 54-May 55	2.5	—1.6	7.7	1.9
5. Sept. 57-Aug. 58	0.0	—8.5	9.9	—0.8
6. Aug. 58-June 59	6.6	3.1	10.5	—0.7

* At annual rates.

TABLE C-13

RUBBER

Sub-Periods	Percentage change in average hourly earnings[*]	Percentage change in production worker employment[*]	Average rate of return on stockholders' equity (after taxes)	Change in rate of return on stockholders' equity (after taxes)[*]
Set I:				
1. Jan. 47-Jan. 49	7.2	−7.0	12.4	−1.8
2. Jan. 49-Oct. 50	3.1	4.1	12.8	5.0
3. Oct. 50-Dec. 53	6.9	−1.2	13.1	−3.6
4. Dec. 53-May 55	5.5	3.8	10.6	1.1
5. May 55-Sept. 57	4.3	−1.6	11.1	−0.8
6. Sept. 57-June 59	4.0	−2.8	10.4	0.1
Set II:				
1. Jan. 49-Nov. 49	0.6	−10.9	8.6	−0.5
2. Nov. 49-Oct. 50	5.3	19.5	14.5	10.0
3. Dec. 53-Sept. 54	2.0	−5.9	10.2	−2.7
4. Sept. 54-May 55	7.6	15.4	11.7	5.5
5. Sept. 57-Aug. 58	4.8	−12.2	9.2	0.4
6. Aug. 58-June 59	3.0	8.5	11.4	−0.5

[*] At annual rates.

TABLE C-14

LEATHER

Sub-Periods	Percentage change in average hourly earnings*	Percentage change in production worker employment*	Average rate of return on stockholders' equity (after taxes)	Change in rate of return on stockholders' equity (after taxes)*
Set I:				
1. Jan. 47-Jan. 49	5.7	—1.9	12.4	—2.0
2. Jan. 49-Oct. 50	4.1	1.0	8.7	4.3
3. Oct. 50-Dec. 53	4.2	—2.4	5.6	—3.8
4. Dec. 53-May 55	1.6	2.1	5.9	2.5
5. May 55-Sept. 57	4.2	—1.6	7.3	—0.3
6. Sept. 57-June 59	2.3	1.0	6.7	1.0
Set II:				
1. Jan. 49-Nov. 49	0.5	—7.4	6.2	0.0
2. Nov. 49-Oct. 50	7.3	9.2	9.0	8.3
3. Dec. 53-Sept. 54	0.0	—0.8	5.0	1.9
4. Sept. 54-May 55	3.3	5.4	7.4	3.7
5. Sept. 57-Aug. 58	0.7	—4.3	5.9	1.6
6. Aug. 58-June 59	3.8	7.2	7.8	0.5

* At annual rates.

TABLE C-15
STONE, CLAY AND GLASS

Sub-Periods	Percentage change in average hourly earnings*	Percentage change in production worker employment*	Average rate of return on stockholders' equity (after taxes)	Change in rate of return on stockholders' equity (after taxes)*
Set I:				
1. Jan. 47-Jan. 49	10.1	−0.3	14.4	0.2
2. Jan. 49-Oct. 50	5.3	5.1	15.4	0.5
3. Oct. 50-Dec. 53	5.6	−1.8	13.1	−2.2
4. Dec. 53-May 55	3.6	1.8	12.4	2.2
5. May 55-Sept. 57	5.6	0.0	18.3	−2.3
6. Sept. 57-June 59	3.6	0.7	11.6	1.1
Set II:				
1. Jan. 49-Nov. 49	2.0	−7.7	13.2	−2.4
2. Nov. 49-Oct. 50	8.2	18.0	16.9	3.1
3. Dec. 53-Sept. 54	1.7	−4.5	11.7	2.1
4. Sept. 54-May 55	4.2	9.0	14.6	4.6
5. Sept. 57-Aug. 58	2.6	−7.6	10.5	1.0
6. Aug. 58-June 59	4.6	10.8	12.9	1.2

* At annual rates.

TABLE C-16
PRIMARY METALS

Sub-Periods	Percentage change in average hourly earnings*	Percentage change in production worker employment*	Average rate of return on stockholders' equity (after taxes)	Change in rate of return on stockholders' equity (after taxes)*
Set I:				
1. Jan. 47-Jan. 49	11.2	0.3	13.3	—2.1
2. Jan. 49-Oct. 50	2.6	0.6	11.9	—0.9
3. Oct. 50-Dec. 53	7.8	—0.7	11.6	—1.9
4. Dec. 53-May 55	3.7	1.3	8.9	0.7
5. May 55-Sept. 57	7.5	—1.0	13.6	—1.3
6. Sept. 57-June 59	6.0	0.2	8.7	—5.0
Set II:				
1. Jan. 49-Nov. 49	—1.1	—39.0	9.3	—12.1
2. Nov. 49-Oct. 50	6.0	54.2	12.7	9.3
3. Dec. 53-Sept. 54	2.2	—13.5	8.6	—4.1
4. Sept. 54-May 55	3.5	19.9	12.2	6.1
5. Sept. 57-Aug. 58	5.6	—20.0	6.5	—3.4
6. Aug. 58-June 59	6.2	27.5	10.2	—6.8

* At annual rates.

TABLE C-17

Fabricated Metals

Sub-Periods	Percentage change in average hourly earnings*	Percentage change in production worker employment*	Average rate of return on stockholders' equity (after taxes)	Change in rate of return on stockholders' equity (after taxes)*
Set I:				
1. Jan. 47-Jan. 49	10.0	—4.0	17.2	—3.6
2. Jan. 49-Oct. 50	4.9	9.6	13.2	0.2
3. Oct. 50-Dec. 53	6.1	—0.9	11.9	—3.0
4. Dec. 53-May 55	3.0	2.8	7.6	—1.3
5. May 55-Sept. 57	5.7	—0.6	10.6	0.5
6. Sept. 57-June 59	4.1	—0.9	7.6	—0.1
Set II:				
1. Jan. 49-Nov. 49	—0.1	—12.0	10.4	—8.6
2. Nov. 49-Oct. 50	9.4	32.5	14.0	8.3
3. Dec. 53-Sept. 54	1.2	—5.5	8.1	—3.1
4. Sept. 54-May 55	3.9	12.4	8.4	4.4
5. Sept. 57-Aug. 58	3.5	—10.9	6.7	—2.4
6. Aug. 58-June 59	4.7	11.2	8.1	2.5

* At annual rates.

TABLE C-18

Machinery (except Electrical)

Sub-Periods	Percentage change in average hourly earnings*	Percentage change in production worker employment*	Average rate of return on stockholders' equity (after taxes)	Change in rate of return on stockholders' equity (after taxes)*
Set I:				
1. Jan. 47-Jan. 49	9.6	-2.5	16.0	-2.4
2. Jan. 49-Oct. 50	4.9	-2.5	12.8	-0.7
3. Oct. 50-Dec. 53	6.6	3.4	12.1	-2.5
4. Dec. 53-May 55	2.5	-3.5	8.6	-0.4
5. May 55-Sept. 57	5.2	2.9	12.1	0.7
6. Sept. 57-June 59	4.6	-4.5	8.2	0.3
Set II:				
1. Jan. 49-Nov. 49	1.1	-25.1	11.6	-8.6
2. Nov. 49-Oct. 50	8.3	24.3	12.5	6.5
3. Dec. 53-Sept. 54	1.1	-11.3	8.8	-1.2
4. Sept. 54-May 55	3.0	5.7	8.2	3.3
5. Sept. 57-Aug. 58	2.8	-21.9	7.1	-3.2
6. Aug. 58-June 59	6.0	18.4	8.4	4.3

* At annual rates.

TABLE C-19

ELECTRICAL MACHINERY

Sub-Periods	Percentage change in average hourly earnings*	Percentage change in production worker employment*	Average rate of return on stockholders' equity (after taxes)	Change in rate of return on stockholders' equity (after taxes)*
Set I:				
1. Jan. 47–Jan. 49	10.1	−7.8	17.6	+0.4
2. Jan. 49–Oct. 50	3.1	12.3	17.2	4.1
3. Oct. 50–Dec. 53	6.2	4.2	14.7	−4.0
4. Dec. 53–May 55	2.3	−3.7	12.4	1.5
5. May 55–Sept. 57	4.8	3.6	12.2	0.3
6. Sept. 57–June 59	4.1	−2.4	11.0	0.4
Set II:				
1. Jan. 49–Nov. 49	−0.4	−13.6	13.5	3.4
2. Nov. 49–Oct. 50	6.3	40.3	19.6	4.8
3. Dec. 53–Sept. 54	.8	−11.3	11.9	−2.1
4. Sept. 54–May 55	3.3	5.6	12.4	2.1
5. Sept. 57–Aug. 58	3.7	−16.0	10.0	−1.3
6. Aug. 58–June 59	4.4	14.8	11.7	2.8

* At annual rates.

TABLE C-20

Transportation Equipment

Sub-Periods	Percentage change in average hourly earnings*	Percentage change in production worker employment*	Average rate of return on stockholders' equity (after taxes)	Change in rate of return on stockholders' equity (after taxes)*
Set I:				
1. Jan. 47-Jan. 49	10.0	-0.8	0.8	5.6
2. Jan. 49-Oct. 50	4.2	6.1	8.9	0.9
3. Oct. 50-Dec. 53	5.8	9.2	11.7	0.5
4. Dec. 53-May 55	3.7	-2.6	16.5	1.7
5. May 55-Sept. 57	4.5	-4.8	15.1	-0.1
6. Sept. 57-June 59	4.9	-2.0	11.7	-1.6
Set II:				
1. Jan. 49-Nov. 49	0.0	-16.8	7.8	-3.8
2. Nov. 49-Oct. 50	8.0	31.3	8.8	5.2
3. Dec. 53-Sept. 54	1.4	-28.1	15.9	+4.5
4. Sept. 54-May 55	4.9	33.1	+6.0	-2.1
5. Sept. 57-Aug. 58	4.5	-20.2	8.4	-7.1
6. Aug. 58-June 59	5.2	22.1	13.4	4.6

* At annual rates.

TABLE C-21

INSTRUMENTS

Sub-Periods	Percentage change in average hourly earnings*	Percentage change in production worker employment*	Average rate of return on stockholders' equity (after taxes)	Change in rate of return on stockholders' equity (after taxes)*
Set I:				
1. Jan. 47-Jan. 49	9.7	−5.4	14.4	−1.2
2. Jan. 49-Oct. 50	5.8	3.7	14.4	1.9
3. Oct. 50-Dec. 53	6.1	6.6	12.7	−2.1
4. Dec. 53-May 55	1.9	−7.9	12.3	1.8
5. May 55-Sept. 57	6.0	2.2	12.5	−0.3
6. Sept. 57-June 59	4.3	−0.2	11.1	1.7
Set II:				
1. Jan. 49-Nov. 49	2.5	−70.8	12.1	−4.3
2. Nov. 49-Oct. 50	8.6	18.4	15.2	6.5
3. Dec. 53-Sept. 54	1.2	−11.1	11.7	2.9
4. Sept. 54-May 55	1.6	−4.8	12.5	−1.6
5. Sept. 57-Aug. 58	4.1	−11.6	10.4	0.5
6. Aug. 58-June 59	4.3	13.7	12.1	2.8

* At annual rates.

Appendix C

TABLE C-22

ALL CIVILIAN EMPLOYEES

Sub-Periods	Percentage change in average annual compensation (including supplements)	Percentage change in total employment
Set I:		
1. Jan. 47-Jan. 49	5.9	1.6
2. Jan. 49-Oct. 50	5.5	4.6
3. Oct. 50-Dec. 53	7.9	—0.6
4. Dec. 53-May 55	3.3	2.5
5. May 55-Sept. 57	5.4	2.2
6. Sept. 57-June 59	4.3	1.4
Set. II:		
1. Jan. 49-Nov. 49	—3.4	4.8
2. Nov. 49-Oct. 50	13.9	4.3
3. Dec. 53-Sept. 54	—0.2	3.2
4. Sept. 54-May 55	7.4	1.6
5. Sept. 57-Aug. 58	2.1	—0.5
6. Aug. 58-June 59	6.6	3.6

APPENDIX D

Concentration and Unionization Ratios

Table D-1 presents concentration ratios for 19 2-digit manufacturing industries for the year 1954. Table D-2 presents unionization ratios for 20 2-digit manufacturing industries for the year 1958. (Ordnance is the 2-digit industry for which a concentration ratio could not be computed.) The sources and methods used in compiling these tables are described below.

Concentration Ratios

Source:

The concentration ratios used here measure the proportion of total shipments in a 4-digit industry made in 1954 by the four largest firms in the industry. (In a few cases, value added was used instead of total shipments.) These data have been taken from: U. S. Senate, Report of the Subcommittee on Antitrust and Monopoly to the Committee on the Judiciary, *Concentration in American Industry,* 85th Cong., 1st Session, 1957, Table 42, pp. 196-219.

Methods:

Since the published concentration ratios measure concentration in 4-digit industries, it was necessary to do some aggregating to obtain concentration ratios for the 2-digit industry groupings used in this study. The aggregation process was carried out by simply averaging the concentration ratios of the 4-digit industries within each 2-digit classification. The proportions of total shipments in the 2-digit industry as a whole that were accounted for by each constituent 4-digit industry were used as weights.[1]

---

[1] This aggregation process probably produces more useful indices of concentration in 2-digit industry groups than would be obtained by simply finding out what proportion of the total shipments of the entire 2-digit industry group were accounted for by the four largest firms. The heterogeneity of some 2-digit industry groupings would make the usual type of non-aggregated concentration ratio a very dubious index of the extent of competition in product markets.

Appendix D

Source:

The unionization ratios presented in Table D-2 measure the percent of workers in each 2-digit manufacturing industry who, in 1958, worked in establishments in which a majority of workers were covered by collective bargaining agreements. The higher the ratio, the higher the degree of unionization. These data have been taken directly from: H. M. Douty, "Collective Bargaining Coverage in Factory Employment, 1958," *Monthly Labor Review,* April 1960, Table 1, p. 347.

TABLE D-1

CONCENTRATION RATIOS FOR 2-DIGIT MANUFACTURING INDUSTRIES
(AS OF 1954)

Industry	Concentration Ratio
Food and kindred products	34
Tobacco manufactures	76
Textile mill products	25
Apparel and other finished textile products	14
Lumber and wood products	10
Furniture and fixtures	17
Paper and allied products	23
Printing, publishing, and allied industries	17
Chemicals and allied products	43
Products of petroleum and coal	35
Rubber products	55
Leather and leather products	27
Stone, clay, and glass products	41
Primary metal industries	49
Fabricated metal products	28
Machinery (except electrical)	31
Electrical machinery	53
Transportation equipment	48
Instruments and related products	43

Appendix D

TABLE D-2

UNIONIZATION RATIOS FOR 2-DIGIT MANUFACTURING INDUSTRIES
(AS OF 1958)

Industry	Unionization Ratio
Ordnance and accessories	83.9
Food and kindred products	68.1
Tobacco manufactures	62.6
Textile mill products	30.1
Apparel and other finished textile products	59.7
Lumber and wood products	43.8
Furniture and fixtures	49.6
Paper and allied products	75.5
Printing, publishing and allied industries	65.3
Chemicals and allied products	65.4
Products of petroleum and coal	89.5
Rubber products	80.6
Leather and leather products	49.3
Stone, clay, and glass products	77.9
Primary metal industries	88.6
Fabricated metal products	70.6
Machinery (except electrical)	67.9
Electrical machinery	72.8
Transportation equipment	86.8
Instruments and related products	51.5

APPENDIX E

Inter-Industry Correlations Between Wage Changes
and Selected Variables, Within Sub-Periods of 1947-59

Tables E-1 and E-2 present simple, partial (first-order, second-order, and third-order), and multiple cross-section correlation coefficients. These coefficients measure the strength of the linear relationship between percentage changes in wages in 19 2-digit manufacturing industries and percentage changes in employment, average levels of profits, concentration ratios, and unionization ratios. Table E-1 presents all these correlation coefficients for the six sub-periods of Set I and Table E-2 presents the results of these same correlations for the six sub-periods of Set II. The usual notations are used in identifying the different types of correlations and the following symbols are used for the variables:

w = percentage change in wages, at an annual rate
e = percentage change in employment, at an annual rate
p = average level of profits
c = concentration ratio
s = unionization ratio

Table E-3 presents the 10%, 5%, 2%, and 1% significance levels for each type of correlation.

Source:

All correlations are based on the data contained in Appendix C and Appendix D. The one 2-digit industry excluded from these correlations because of lack of data is Ordnance.

Appendix E

TABLE E-1

	Set I Sub-Periods					
Correlation Coefficients	(I.1) Jan. 47- Jan. 49	(I.2) Jan. 49- Oct. 50	(I.3) Oct. 50- Dec. 53	(I.4) Dec. 53- May 55	(I.5) May 55- Sept. 57	(I.6) Sept. 57- May 59
r_{we}	.48	.19	.44	—.04	.22	—.49
$r_{we.p}$	.51	.14	.23	—.14	.19	—.33
$r_{we.c}$	.49	.16	.23	—.18	.42	.09
$r_{we.s}$	.52	.17	.17	—.18	.27	—.45
$r_{we.cs}$	.66	.14	.05	—.23	.90	.10
$r_{we.cp}$	.73	.28	.09	—.19	.50	.09
$r_{we.sp}$	.51	.11	.04	—.19	.30	—.34
$r_{we.csp}$	.82	.06	—.03	—.23	.90	.08
r_{wp}	.21	.36	.64	.49	.18	.60
$r_{wp.e}$	.33	.34	.55	.51	.14	.50
$r_{wp.c}$	.24	.40	.54	.06	.33	.03
$r_{wp.s}$	.28	.44	.53	.33	—.07	.58
$r_{wp.ce}$	.64	.38	.51	.08	.43	—.02
$r_{wp.cs}$	.29	.40	.38	.00	.13	.06
$r_{wp.se}$	.25	.43	.40	.35	—.17	.51
$r_{wp.cse}$	.68	.38	.38	.00	.09	.01
r_{wc}	—.06	—.14	.54	.69	—.17	.72
$r_{wc.e}$	.11	—.09	.41	.70	—.39	.61
$r_{wc.p}$	.10	—.22	.39	.56	—.32	.50
$r_{wc.s}$	—.08	.03	.33	.62	—.44	.71
$r_{wc.ep}$	.55	—.19	.34	.57	—.55	.41
$r_{wc.sp}$	.08	—.03	.27	.55	—.45	.52
$r_{wc.es}$	.37	—.08	.29	.63	—.84	.62
$r_{wc.sep}$	.68	—.18	.25	.56	—.84	.41

Appendix E

Correlation Coefficients	SET I SUB-PERIODS					
	(I.1) Jan. 47- Jan. 49	(I.2) Jan. 49- Oct. 50	(I.3) Oct. 50- Dec. 53	(I.4) Dec. 53- May 55	(I.5) May 55- Sept. 57	(I.6) Sept. 57- May 59
r_{ws}	.02	—.36	.74	.41	.41	.22
$r_{ws.e}$	—.22	—.35	.68	.44	.44	.07
$r_{ws.p}$	.18	—.44	.61	.24	.38	—.08
$r_{ws.c}$	.05	—.34	.66	.14	.56	—.18
$r_{ws.ep}$	—.04	—.44	.59	.21	.45	—.15
$r_{ws.ec}$	—.52	—.33	.64	.20	.94	—.18
$r_{ws.pc}$	.17	—.40	.56	.13	.49	—.19
$r_{ws.epc}$	—.23	—.40	.56	.18	.62	—.19
$r_{w.pe}$	.54	.38	.66	.51	.26	.66
$r_{w.cs}$	.08	.37	.78	.70	.58	.73
$r_{w.pc}$	.25	.42	.71	.69	.37	.72
$r_{w.se}$	.52	.39	.75	.44	.48	.49
$r_{w.ce}$	.49	.21	.57	.70	.45	.72
$r_{w.sp}$	.28	.55	.82	.51	.42	.61
$r_{w.cse}$	.66	.42	.78	.72	.94	.73
$r_{w.pec}$	.74	.43	.71	.71	.59	.72
$r_{w.csp}$	.55	.52	.81	.70	.59	.73
$r_{w.pes}$	.56	.55	.82	.53	.50	.67
$r_{w.espc}$	.84	.55	.82	.72	.94	.73
$r^2_{w.espc}$	.71	.30	.67	.52	.88	.53

Appendix E

TABLE E-2

RESULTS OF CORRELATION ANALYSIS:
SET II SUB-PERIODS

Correlation Coefficients	SET II SUB-PERIODS					
	(II.1) Jan. 49- Nov. 49	*(II.2)* Nov. 49- Oct. 50	*(II.3)* Dec. 53- Sept. 54	*(II.4)* Sept. 54- May 55	*(II.5)* Sept. 57- Aug. 58	*(II.6)* Aug. 58- June 59
r_{we}	—.11	.35	—.12	—.06	—.30	—.10
$r_{we.p}$	—.11	.33	.10	—.24	—.27	—.28
$r_{we.c}$	—.08	.52	—.18	—.32	.18	—.29
$r_{we.s}$	—.16	.73	.08	—.18	—.22	—.15
$r_{we.cs}$	—.13	.88	—.04	—.25	.14	—.26
$r_{we.cp}$	—.09	.47	.07	—.28	.13	—.23
$r_{we.sp}$	—.19	.72	.14	—.35	—.33	—.27
$r_{we.csp}$	—.16	.87	.12	—.14	.15	—.21
r_{wp}	.10	.12	.31	.27	.61	.31
$r_{wp.e}$	.10	—.02	.30	.35	.60	.40
$r_{wp.c}$	.08	.24	.50	—.33	.14	.22
$r_{wp.s}$	.13	.22	.10	.22	.58	.29
$r_{wp.ce}$	.10	.07	.48	—.21	.06	—.12
$r_{wp.cs}$	.11	.27	.36	—.29	.02	—.20
$r_{wp.se}$	.16	.48	.20	—.44	.62	—.37
$r_{wp.cse}$	.15	—.13	.37	—.21	—.08	—.12
r_{wc}	.09	—.36	—.07	.70	.73	.51
$r_{wc.e}$	.04	—.52	—.15	.73	.71	.56
$r_{wc.p}$	.06	—.41	—.41	.71	.52	.47
$r_{wc.s}$	.14	—.20	—.31	.71	.83	.52
$r_{wc.ep}$	.00	—.52	—.40	.71	.48	.45
$r_{wc.sp}$	.11	—.26	—.45	.72	.55	.48
$r_{wc.es}$	.09	—.39	—.30	.72	.83	.55
$r_{wc.sep}$	.05	—.55	—.55	.64	.72	.45

Appendix E

Correlation Coefficients	(II.1) Jan. 49-Nov. 49	(II.2) Nov. 49-Oct. 50	(II.3) Dec. 53-Sept. 54	(II.4) Sept. 54-May 55	(II.5) Sept. 57-Aug. 58	(II.6) Aug. 58-June 59
r_{ws}	—.07	—.43	.40	.18	.23	.11
$r_{ws.e}$	—.14	—.78	.39	.25	.11	.16
$r_{ws.p}$	—.11	—.46	.28	.07	—.05	—.04
$r_{ws.c}$	—.13	—.32	.49	—.22	—.18	—.16
$r_{ws.ep}$	—.19	—.78	.30	.18	—.21	.02
$r_{ws.ec}$	—.16	—.85	.46	—.09	—.14	—.09
$r_{ws.pc}$	—.14	—.34	.34	—.16	—.20	—.13
$r_{ws.epc}$	—.19	—.74	.36	—.08	—.16	—.08
$r_{w.pe}$	.15	.35	.32	.35	.65	.41
$r_{w.cs}$	.16	.47	.49	.72	.74	.53
$r_{w.pc}$	.12	.42	.50	.74	.74	.54
$r_{w.se}$	.18	.81	.42	.26	.32	.19
$r_{w.ce}$	.12	.60	.19	.73	.74	.57
$r_{w.sp}$	.15	.47	.41	.28	.61	.31
$r_{w.cse}$	.20	.91	.49	.73	.75	.57
$r_{w.pec}$	.15	.61	.50	.75	.74	.58
$r_{w.csp}$	.19	.53	.59	.75	.74	.56
$r_{w.pes}$	.24	.81	.43	.39	.67	.41
$r_{w.espc}$	.24	.91	.59	.75	.75	.58
$r^2_{w.espc}$	.06	.83	.35	.56	.56	.34

TABLE E-3
SIGNIFICANCE LEVELS OF THE COEFFICIENT OF CORRELATION*

Correlation Coefficients	LEVELS OF SIGNIFICANCE			
	10%	5%	2%	1%
r_{12}	.389	.456	.528	.575
$r_{12.3}$	.400	.468	.542	.590
$r_{12.34}$	.412	.482	.558	.605
$r_{12.345}$	.426	.497	.574	.623
$r_{1.23}$	.50	.55	.61	.66
$r_{1.234}$	.58	.63	.67	.72
$r_{1.2345}$	.65	.71	.75	.80

* N=19 throughout.

RESEARCH PROJECTS OF THE INDUSTRIAL RELATIONS
SECTION

The Wage-Price Issue. A Theoretical Analysis. By William G. Bowen. 1960. 447 pp. $8.50. (Published by Princeton University Press.)

Management in the Industrial World. An International Analysis. By Frederick Harbison and Charles A. Myers. 1959. 413 pp. $7.00, (Published by McGraw-Hill Book Company.)

Authority and Organization in German Management. By Heinz Hartmann. 1959. 318 pp. $6.00. (Published by Princeton University Press.)

Human Resources for Egyptian Enterprise. By Frederick Harbison and Ibrahim A. Ibrahim. 1958. 230 pp. $5.50. (Published by McGraw-Hill Book Company.)

As Unions Mature. An Analysis of the Evolution of American Unionism. By Richard A. Lester. 1958. 171 pp. $3.75. (Published by Princeton University Press.)

Reports
(Published by the Industrial Relations Section)

Wage Behavior in the Postwar Period. An Empirical Analysis. Report Series No. 100. 1960. 139 pp. $3.00.

The Scientist in American Industry. Some organizational determinants in manpower utilization. Report Series No. 99. 1960. 160 pp. $3.00.

High-Level Manpower in Overseas Subsidiaries. Experience in Brazil and Mexico. Report Series No. 98. 1960. 161 pp. $3.00.

Unions in America. A British view. Report Series No. 97. 1959. 136 pp. $2.00.

Manpower and Innovation in American Industry. Report Series No. 96. 1959. 85 pp. $2.00.

High-Talent Manpower for Science and Industry. An appraisal of policy at home and abroad. Report Series No. 95. 1957. 98 pp. $3.00.

Codetermination in the German Steel Industry. Report Series No. 94. 1956. 114 pp. $3.50.

Disability Retirement in Industrial Pension Plans. Report Series No. 93. 1956. 62 pp. $2.00.

Union Strike Votes. Current practice and proposed controls. Report Series No. 92. 1956. 141 pp. $3.00.

Bibliographies

Manpower Problems in Economic Development. Bibliographical Series No. 85. 1958. 93 pp. $2.00.

Incentive Wage Systems. Bibliographical Series No. 83. (Revised) 1956. 24 pp. 50 cents.

A Trade Union Library. Bibliographical Series No. 84. 1955. (Revised) 58 pp. $1.50.

Complete list of available publications will be sent on request.